Table of Contents

childhood years and is a true mental disorder. ADHD can affect the way children think, feel and act. Almost all children are inattentive and overactive from time to time, but for children suffering with ADHD and their families, their behavior is often disruptive and extreme.

ADHD affects approximately five percent of school age children. Overall, ADHD is about four times more common in boys. In some children, there is a period of remission around puberty time, but for others, the condition left untreated can continue throughout their adult life.

In general, a child with ADHD has a hard time concentrating, is constantly moving around and might have a poor performance at school compared with intelligence. Oftentimes, their behavior at school or home is disruptive.

Below are some of the symptoms of ADHD that manifests in infants

They are constantly thirsty.

They experience extreme restlessness, sleep patterns and crying.

They are difficult to feed.

They have frequent tantrums, rocking the bed and head banging.

Some of the ADHD symptoms in older children are below.

They have a brief attention span and poor concentration.

They are impulsive, and do not stop to think.

They have poor coordination.

They lack self-esteem

They are always on the go.

They take undue risks and seem fearless.

They have a weaker short-term memory

They have sleeping and eating problems.

Not every infant or child with ADHD will have these features, and the degrees of severity can vary from child to child.

There are three types of ADHD:

Predominately Inattentive ADHD – This type of ADHD is when a person has a very hard time organizing and finishing up a task. They have a hard time following instructions and listening to conversations. They find it too hard to pay attention to all the details of a task.

Predominantly Hyperactive-Impulsive Type – With this type of ADHD, a person has a hard time keeping still. They are constantly talking and fidgeting around. Smaller children will jump, run and climb continually. They are impulsive and restless – constantly interrupting others, talking when it is inappropriate and grabbing things. They cannot wait for their turn, and they have more accidents and injuries than others do.

Combined Type – A person who has symptoms of both is considered to have the combined type of ADHD.

It is pretty well accepted that a child with ADHD lacks the ability to focus their attention on one thing at a time, that they are impulsive and that oftentimes, they cannot control motor access. These deficits can create a dysfunctional performance at school, at home and socially.

Children with ADHD might require more monitoring from teachers and parents due to the lack of internal neurological control. This will better help them adapt to their inefficiencies.

When ADHD is diagnosed early in a child's life, it is easier to begin developing an effective system of monitoring strategies which help prevent any further complications. When a child is not diagnosed accurately or in the early stages, there is a pretty good chance that teachers and parents both will experience some frustration and possibly even become angry with the child.

Equally, the child may experience feelings of frustration and anger as well as developing low self-esteem.

There is not a formal test to diagnose ADHD, so information such as evaluations, observations and information from the parents, teachers, mental health professionals and physicians are used. Listed below is some of the information used to make a diagnosis of the condition.

Parent Interview – A parent interview gives specific information about pregnancy and birth of the child. Giving the doctor descriptions of the child's temperament can reveal certain characteristics of problematic social behavior and poor neurological structure. The medical history of the child and parents as well as other family members might rule out another condition or unmask something associated with ADHD. Having a long discussion with the family offers a better understanding of the dynamics going on inside the child's home.

Teacher Interview – Information the school provides might give a clean perspective of the way the child is functioning, where a parent might be more emotionally influenced when making their observations. The school setting offers a good gauge to judge the character of the child. The evaluator will talk to the teacher about how the child deals with daily work demands and routine compared to other children. When the evaluation is complete, it might be determined that the child has a disability learning which displays some of the same characteristics of ADHD.

Physician Evaluation – An evaluation by a physician is needed to understand behavioral and developmental issues in children. Because ADHD is neurological, a complete assessment of the child's neurological system is necessary. Clinical evaluations might identify some inadequacies or dysfunctions that influence the child's performance. Having a combination of findings from the parent, school and physician will allow a diagnosis of ADHD versus other possible conditions.

Parents should assist their ADHD child with understanding the strengths and weaknesses he has. Part of the child's treatment might include teaching and parenting changes to assist the child with their weaknesses.

Medication is another avenue of treatment used for ADHD. The limitations, expectations and side effects of all medications for treating

ADHD should be evaluated. The understanding when using medication for ADHD is that the medicine is not a cure for ADHD – all is vital.

The parents and teachers of an ADHD child need to send a message to the child that their difficulties are understood and that they are both willing to provide assistance and support for the ADHD. They should also let the ADHD child know that a commitment is expected from him or her as well. Cooperation, communication and compromise will help everyone reach this goal.

Chapter 2- Does ADHD Impact Relationships

As the years have progressed, you have learned a lot more about ADHD and the impact that it can have on the person who is dealing with it. However, you might not know as much about how ADHD can actually impact relationships. The short answer is yes, it can impact all different types of relationships. How exactly does this happen?

Making Friends

You might think that issues with making friends are something relegated to the domain of childhood. Little ones do not necessarily understand what ADHD is, and they might not be willing to befriend someone who is suffering from it. While this might be true in some cases, adults are probably more likely to shy away from someone is different than they are. Children tend to be more welcoming. However, at all ages, making friends can be difficult for someone who has ADHD in general.

Not Sharing Information

Relationships can also be difficult because people with ADHD do not always want to share information about their condition. They do not want to let people know that they have this condition. As a result, other individuals do not always understand what is going on. They might feel that the other person is hiding something, or they might suspect that the other person has ADHD. However, people need to understand that individuals who have ADHD will come around when they are ready to. It is important not to push people into sharing details that they are uncomfortable with.

Creating a Level of Secrecy

Due to this secrecy, however, it can be difficult for a bond to really form. The people who have ADHD might feel bad that they are keeping secrets from their new friends, and the others can feel that secrets are being kept. Trust is a very important part of a relationship, and it might be hard for people to reach this level when everything is not out in the open. This is also extremely important for a romantic relationship. It just may take a little bit longer to develop in this type of situation than in other ones.

Fear of Judgment

When we have relationships with people, we should not be afraid that they are going to judge us. Yet, even with some of our good friends, we wonder if we are being judged for the things we do, the words we say, the clothes we wear and so forth. Still though, just imagine how much stronger this fear of judgment would be if you had ADHD. You might be worrying that people are constantly talking about the condition that you have and that people are making assumptions about you based off of this diagnosis.

Fear of ADHD

Unfortunately, too many people do not understand what ADHD is. They just throw this term around like it is nothing, and they do not take the time to find out more about the condition. They are really doing a disservice to people who have ADHD. If someone who is uneducated and ignorant about ADHD meets someone who has the condition, the first individual might have some preconceived notions. This person might make assumptions about the other individual and not even allow a relationship to develop. This is quite a sad situation indeed, and we must work to rectify it in society.

Having to Treat ADHD

Some people do not have any patience for things that are outside of their realm of existence. Having to treat ADHD is something they might not understand at all. People who are suffering from ADHD could be utilizing a variety of methods to deal with the issues. They might be taking medications, or they may be going to specialists to work out all of their problems. However, the other people in the relationship might not understand these necessities. They might wonder why it just cannot be about them all of the time.

ADHD That's Not Diagnosed

Now, let's say that a relationship is starting between two people. They might really like each other, and they may be spending a lot more time with each other. With all of this time, one member is starting to notice that something seems to be bothering the other person. The second individual never wants to talk about it, and he or she does not even want to acknowledge that there is an issue. As a result, the couple tends to get into a lot of fights and arguments about it. What could the problem be? Well, it might be ADHD that has never been diagnosed.

In an Educational Setting

We should pay some attention to how ADHD can affect relationships in an educational setting. Students might not understand why others in their class act a certain way. Teachers not trained in special education may not know what to do when they have a student who has ADHD in their classrooms. On top of that, students with ADHD might have a lot of trouble working with groups. Fortunately, schools are becoming more vigilant about all of these issues, and they are working to ensure cohesion throughout and to craft plans to address the needs of specific students.

As you can see, ADHD definitely does impact relationships. That is not even really the main question anymore. At this point, you need to understand how ADHD can impact relationships and what can be done to better handle these types of issues.

Chapter 3- ADHD in Marriage and Romantic Relationships What You Should Know

Many people associate ADHD with childhood and a hyperactive kid that runs around the room, bouncing off the walls, much to his mother's dismay. However, attention deficit hyperactivity disorder doesn't just go away when a person hits adulthood. Although the likelihood that an adult can control their behavior increases with age, the disorder remains and may cause problems in relationships.

Researchers suggest that people who suffer from ADHD have an increased chance to experience problems in their most important relationships such as divorce. ADHD can even cause problems in relationships where marriage is not yet a factor. Although living with ADHD in a relationship or marriage often requires extra work, a successful relationship is possible even with this disorder.

Common Behaviors of ADHD and the Impact It Has On Relationships

People in a relationship don't always communicate clearly or often enough and this problem is often amplified when a person has ADHD. A partner might feel that a person is distracted all the time because he or she doesn't care when it's actually a product of ADHD. People who are distracted all the time might seem distant and uncaring, and to prevent a relationship from disintegrating, it's necessary to understand the general characteristics of people who live with ADHD.

Some of the most common attributes of someone who has ADHD is the incredible distractibility of the person. Not only does this naturally distracted nature lead to unfinished projects, but this symptom might also cause a person to forget things. In a relationship, this might mean forgetting something important like an anniversary or forgetting something minor like returning a video to the store.

People with ADHD are also likely to ignore directions and try to accomplish projects without the input of anyone else. They may reject the advice and suggestions of others, which may cause problems in a relationship when a partner just wants to help. Such behavior might make it seem as though the individual with ADHD doesn't appreciate the input of his or her partner. This is why communication is so important in a relationship when someone has ADHD.

The tendency of a person with ADHD to fidget and squirm may seem annoying to his or her partner, but fidgeting shouldn't be interpreted as a signal that someone doesn't want to be there and wants to do something else. Someone who taps his foot during a children's school recital due to his ADHD isn't necessarily interested in being elsewhere. The fidgeting is simply a common symptom or characteristic of someone who has ADHD and must sit still for a long period of time.

People with ADHD are also very likely to be incredibly talkative and likely to interrupt conversations or try to take over the discussion. This isn't a sign of impatience with a partner; excitement during conversations is simply the result of a hyperactive nature and a need to be talking, moving, or fidgeting all the time. Getting used to a person's inappropriate comments and loudness may be difficult for a partner who isn't used to acting with such exuberance all the time.

How to Live With a Person Who Has ADHD

Although people who have ADHD may have problems sustaining long-term relationships and marriage, it's not impossible to be happy with such an individual as long as that person's partner knows about the condition and how to deal with it in a relationship. One of the problems that commonly results from such relationships is that one person in the relationship tries the same thing over and over again and doesn't get the result he or she wants.

For example, a person might try to remind his or her partner on a daily basis about something important, but the knowledge never seems to stick. Instead of getting frustrated with a partner's behavior, it's better to consider a different approach to the problem. It's possible that a verbal reminder just isn't the right way to make sure a person with ADHD remembers something. Trying a different angle, such as writing something down, may provide a much better reminder. People with ADHD tend to forget things they're told almost immediately yet may be able to deal much better with a written reminder.

It's impossible to understand motives without communication in a typical relationship, but this issue could be greatly exaggerated in a relationship where someone has ADHD. An extraordinary amount of tension may build if there isn't effort on the part of both members in the relationship or marriage to communicate regularly. It's essential that someone without ADHD doesn't blame the other person in the relationship for their behavior.

Learning to live in harmony with a person who has ADHD does take a lot of effort, and it's not something that can be dealt with a single time. ADHD is a lifelong condition and requires smart planning on the part of the person who doesn't have ADHD and effort on the part of the person suffering from the condition. Living with someone who has ADHD can be frustrating, but it can also be exciting and constantly surprising.

A person who has ADHD must certainly work hard to ensure the success of any relationship; however, his or her partner must also entertain creative strategies for a successful relationship. ADHD is a condition that may impact anyone and is common across all age groups, genders, and socioeconomic backgrounds. A successful relationship certainly isn't impossible when one of the members has ADHD, but it does require extra attention paid to communication since the natural behavior of someone with

ADHD may appear as incredibly insensitive or unloving to the person who doesn't have ADHD.

Chapter 4- Dating and Marriage Strains

Romantic relationships are some of the most fulfilling relationships that a person can enjoy in life. However, these relationships are also the most challenging. There is no such thing as a perfect relationship. Even the best dating or marriage partnership is the union of two imperfect people.

Each relationship is different, but there are some common strains that will affect almost every couple during some point in their journey together. If you are aware of these strains, you can be proactive in protecting your relationship.

A Crammed Schedule

We are living in a busy and harried world. Your task list is most likely filled to the brim, and there are always more tasks and people that need something from you.

A crammed schedule can place a tremendous strain on a relationship. When you are too busy, you do not have adequate time to spend with your partner. A lack of time turns into a lack of communication, and it is easy for your relationship to fall into a downward spiral.

If your schedule or your partner's schedule is affecting your relationship, something has to give. You continue at such a frantic place for the long term without growing apart.

If you desire to free up some time in your schedule, sit down with a piece of paper and write down your normal daily schedule. Take a look at each item on the list, and try to find just one thing that you can eliminate. After you eliminate that item, you can start eliminating other unnecessary tasks.

Money

Money is one of the most common factors that cause disagreements between couples. If you are dating, it can be tricky to figure out who should pay on dates. If you are married, the financial decisions are even more important.

In many relationships, one person is a saver and the other is a spender. This difference can be the source of tension, but it can also be an asset in your relationship. Instead of fighting against your differences, try to find some common ground. You can set guidelines for money that will keep both parties happy.

For instance, you might decide that you will consult the other person when you are making a purchase over $100. This allows the spender to have some freedom in how she spends her money, and it also allows the saver to be assured that he will be consulted before large purchases.

Growing and Changing

Whether you start a relationship when you are 15 or 50, you never stop changing. As you have new life experiences, you will be continually growing and changing. Some of these changes will be positive, and some will be negative, but changes are an inevitable part of romantic relationships.

If you are not prepared for changes in your relationship, they can shake you to your core. It is disconcerting to realize the person that you married has evolved into a different person. When you are feeling disheartened by changes, be honest with your partner. The dynamics of your relationship will change many times throughout the decades that you spend together, but change can actually be a very good thing.

Other People

Even though you are involved in a romantic relationship, you still have many other relationships in your life. Your friends, co-workers and family members might all have an opinion about your relationship, but it is important to set boundaries.

This is especially true in the first few years after your marriage. Your parents can still be an important part of your lives, but they need to respect the fact that your spouse is now your number one priority.

Other people can put a tremendous strain on your relationship, but they can only do this if you let them. If your friends are constantly saying negative things about your spouse, it might be time to put some distance between you and them. If your co-worker is still flirting with you after your wedding, let him know that this behavior is not acceptable.

It can be uncomfortable to set boundaries with other people, but it is a necessary step in protecting your relationship.

Different Priorities

During different seasons in your life, your priorities can shift from your relationship to other areas. When you have a lot of obligations at work, your job can become your number one priority.

Once children enter your family, it is easy to place more value on your relationships with your children than on your relationship with your spouse. Young children require a lot of time and effort, but this does not mean that you have to neglect your relationship. The quantity of time that you spend with your spouse will change many times throughout your marriage, but the quality of time does not have to vary.

When you are feeling overwhelmed, sit down with your partner and make a list of your priorities. If your marriage is your top priority, discuss how you can find time to spend together. It can be as elaborate as a special vacation away together or as simple as an at-home date night with pizza and dessert after the kids are in bed for the night.

You will likely experience these strains and many others in your romantic relationships, but these strains do not have to tear you apart. Instead, they can help you grow stronger.

Chapter 5- What Are Adult ADHD Symptoms

Some people think of ADHD as a disorder that affects children and adolescents. However, ADHD is also prevalent among adults. Many adults have been dealing with ADHD throughout their lifetime without proper diagnosis and help.

If you suspect that you or someone you care about could be suffering from ADHD, consider the following symptoms. All of these symptoms will not occur in every patient, but most ADHD sufferers will display at least several of these traits.

Problems with Distraction

Distractions can be brutal to a person with ADHD. We are living in a noisy and busy world. For a person with ADHD, the amount of distractions can keep them from being able to complete their daily tasks.

For instance, a person with ADHD who works in an office environment might be so distracted by co-workers phone calls that he cannot focus on writing an e-mail. This makes it difficult to complete important tasks in a timely manner.

Lack of Organization

A person with ADHD often finds it very difficult to get organized and stay organized. Difficulty organizing tasks is one of the most common complaints among adults with ADHD. At times, this can just be a nuisance, such as when a person misplaces their car keys on regular basis.

However, in some instances, a lack of organization can have serious consequences. Bills that are not paid on time can result in significant late fees. When a person with ADHD becomes a parent, a lack of organization and focus can even put their child in a dangerous situation.

Relationship Issues

Relationships are not always easy, and this is especially true when one or both parties is dealing with ADHD. Many of the symptoms of ADHD, such as missing commitments, an inability to concentrate and poor listening skills, can be difficult to deal with in a relationship. These things can unwittingly signal to your partner that you do not care about the relationship.

Since a person with ADHD feels that these traits are normal, it can be difficult for her to understand why her partner is so upset. This cycle can continue and cause numerous problems in a relationship.

Traffic Tickets

You might be wondering what in the world traffic tickets have to do with a mental disorder, but the two are actually correlated. Safe driving requires concentration and focus, two things that are very difficult for someone with ADHD to accomplish on a consistent basis.

For instance, a person with ADHD can be so distracted by a flashing light on a sign near the road that he rear ends the car in front of him. If you regularly receive speeding tickets or traffic violations, it can be a sign of ADHD.

Anger Issues

We all have angry outbursts from time to time. A reasonable amount of anger is normal, but anger can be more pronounced in an adult with ADHD. Some ADHD suffers report that they do not feel like they are in control over their emotions. Therefore, angry outbursts can occur after seemingly minor offenses.

After an angry outburst, the anger can subside as quickly as it erupted. However, these outbursts can have long term negative effects on both business and personal relationships.

Poor Time Management

Are you almost always late for events? Have you missed important deadlines at work? Does your spouse complain that you are not keeping your promises? If so, your ADHD could be manifesting itself in poor time management.

Adults with ADHD can have a difficult time managing their time in an effective manner. This can result from a lack of concentration and focus. It can also occur because the person is easily distracted.

Restlessness

Many adults with ADHD complain that they regularly have a feeling of restlessness, even when they desperately want to unwind and relax. The hyperactivity part of ADHD is sometimes overlooked, but it can be a difficult symptom for patients to handle.

At times, these people are described as being overly tense or grouchy by their loved ones. However, their minds keep racing, resulting in the inability to relax. This can also affect their sleep habits and cause exhaustion.

Unbalanced Priorities

Finally, an adult with ADHD can be criticized for not having the right priorities. Some families report that the family member with ADHD misses important events even after he has been repeatedly reminded.

A young adult with ADHD might become so engrossed in video games that he misses a crucial meeting at work. ADHD can cause a person to lose the ability to correctly prioritize. Therefore, they give more precedence to unimportant things while missing things that have a major effect on their lives.

If several of these symptoms describe you or someone that you love, make an appointment with your physician. Only a medical professional can provide a valid ADHD diagnosis. When you meet with your physician, he will ask you to answer a list of questions about your behavior. It is important to be honest during your consultation so that the doctor can provide an accurate diagnosis.

It can be intimidating to hear that you have a disorder, but knowledge is power. There are many different treatments available to help those who are suffering with ADHD. Prescription medication is not the only solution. Many ADHD sufferers find relief through counseling or behavior modification sessions.

Chapter 6- How to Improve a Relationship When One Person Has ADHD

Do you feel like ADHD is having a huge negative impact on your relationship? Perhaps your partner has ADHD, and it is causing a lot of problems and stressing both of you out to the point that the relationship may fail. Rather than giving up on it, there are some things that you can do to improve the relationship. All is not yet lost. It will take work and dedication on your part, but it can be done. Below are a few tips and tricks that you can use, and you should see immediate improvement in your relationship.

First of all, you need to remember that your partner has a medical condition that is changing the way that he or she acts. If your boyfriend or husband has ADHD, do not think that he is acting this way to annoy you or because he does not care about you. It is a documented medical case with clear correlations to the way that the brain and body work together. Once you get your head around this fact, it makes it easier to be patient and to work hard to make the situation better, just like you would if he had any other medical issue.

Next, you should talk to the doctor about ADHD medication and your different options in that realm. There could be a simple pill that he can take that will alter the way that he feels, instantly improving the way that he acts. Many people forget that ADHD really can be treated. He does not necessarily just have to fight through it all on his own. With the right medication, the whole thing may become far less of a struggle for the two of you, and you can then start to grow close once again.

Additionally, studies have shown that many of the chemicals in modern food can be linked to ADHD. This is not to say that the chemicals cause it, per se, but they can certainly make it worse. In particular, the links have been found with preservatives, artificial flavors, and artificial colors. Try switching over to a diet of natural foods that have not been processed. Even buying organic fruits and vegetables can help. In some cases, it has even been shown that people who change over to this type of a diet do not also need to take the medications in order to fight off the symptoms of ADHD.

Now that you know how to understand and treat the disorder, there are things that you can do to improve your relationship even when he stays the same. For starters, try doing more things that he enjoys, things that keep him occupied. You may think that going to the opera sounds like a romantic date night, but the fact of the matter is that some people just have a very hard time concentrating for that long. If you change the things that you do, you will have more fun together and you will enjoy going out on dates.

Another thing that you have probably noticed is that people with ADHD tend to forget about things. They do not do this because they do not care about those things, but they just have a tendency to slip their minds. They may have been planning on doing it, but then they got distracted by something and went off and did that instead. This can cause an incredible amount of stress in a relationship when the forgotten things are mortgage payments or anniversary dinner plans. What can you do to keep this situation from happening?

The best thing to do, as the person who does not have ADHD, is to realize that you have strengths that the other person lacks. You are better at some things, naturally, than they are. This is not a bad thing. All people are different. You just need to know how to use your strengths. Take the time to write everything on the calendar. Put notes around the house when you want to make sure that something gets done. If you think he is going to forget, do not be afraid to call and remind him. With a little extra effort, you can balance things out and reduce the stress in your relationship.

You may think that this is not fair to you, and you would be right. It is not fair. However, a relationship, just like life, is not always going to be fair. The relationships that last are the ones in which both parties are committed to making them last. You need to put in the work and the effort, not just expecting everything to work out on its own. This positive action can really change the way that the two of you relate. He will appreciate it, and you can be sure that he will show it by doing things to help you out as well.

If you do all of this, your relationship will really grow and evolve. It could become stronger than it ever would have been if you had both entered it without ADHD. Your compassionate assistance is going to endear you to your boyfriend or your husband. He will be very grateful that you helped him out when he needed it, and he will love you all the more for it. Try out some of these things as soon as you can if you want to see positive changes.

Chapter 7- How to Treat ADHD

ADHD, short for attention deficit hyperactivity disorder, seems to be diagnosed more and more these days. A lot of people are noticing a spike in the number of individuals who have it, and they are wondering what is going on. Well, in the mean time, individuals need to learn how to treat ADHD in a person.

Taking Courses on the Subject

When you want to learn how to treat ADHD in people, you need to be really dedicated to the discipline. You cannot learn all of the information that you need to know in a short article. No, instead, you should enroll in some classes. Courses offered at colleges that teach prospective teachers how to work with students who have learning disabilities would be the best idea. Generally, you are going to want to enroll in some sort of higher education program if you really want to learn how to work with people who have ADHD.

Gain Practical Experience

Learning how to treat ADHD is so much more than taking courses although these are a seriously important part of the process. When you want to learn how to treat ADHD in a person, you are going to have to gain practical experience in the field. If you are in a college program, it's really important that you are signing up for internships. You may be able to work in hospitals or other treatment facilities to learn the appropriate methods to use. So many different types of methods can be used these days to address such issues.

Learning Who Can Be Affected

Right now, you might have a fairly narrow scope when it comes to understanding who can be affected by ADHD. You must understand that anyone can fall into this category. Yes, we often hear about children who have ADHD. Perhaps this is because educational systems are focusing more on learning disabilities, or maybe it is because more people are being diagnosed as children. Still, so many adults are struggling with ADHD as well. You need to learn the methods appropriate for handling both of these populations in the ways that are most effective for them.

Identifying the Signs and Symptoms of ADHD

Before you can begin to treat a person with ADHD, you need to know that the person definitely has it. Be very careful about how you approach this. Depending upon your position and job title, you might not have the authority to diagnosis anyone with anything. Even if you think you know what the issue is, you may be unable to make any sort of formal declarations. An array of different symptoms is found in people with ADHD. You will likely notice that the person has a lot of trouble staying still and paying attention.

Understanding the Level of Severity

When you are selecting a treatment program for a person who has been diagnosed with ADHD, you need to understand how severe the case is. People who have very mild forms might be able to function perfectly in a regular classroom or group setting. They might need a reminder from time-to-time about sitting quietly. On the other side, some individuals might have very severe forms. Children may have to be in certain schools that are equipped to provide them with the best educational and learning experiences as are possible.

Knowing Someone Who Has ADHD

Perhaps you are not necessarily looking for advice on such a sophisticated medical level. Maybe you have a person in your life who is suffering from ADHD, and you are not quite sure how to act around that individual. Well, you should act as you always have. The individual is likely self-conscious about it, and you do not want to make him or her feel even worse. Just remember that you are likely going to have to exercise a great deal of patience. When you truly care about a person, this should not be a huge sacrifice for you to make.

Thinking You Have ADHD

It's also possible that you believe you might have ADHD yourself, and you are not sure how you can deal with it or where to turn. Remaining calm is important. Yes, you can look up some of the signs and symptoms, but you do not want to get all worried for nothing. The first thing to do is to schedule appointments with your doctor or a counselor. Other factors could be at the heart of your issues, and you want to ensure that you are getting the proper treatment.

Picking Treatment Plans for Yourself

Always remember that suggestions are not supposed to take the place of medical advice. When you want to know how to treat ADHD in another person or in yourself, you need to be sure you are working with a professional. These are the individuals who will let you know what needs to be done, how the plans can be executed and what the safety risks are, if any. Without this type of professional advice, you could make a mistake. If you hope to be a professional in the field, you need to take the correct steps to get to that point.

Treating ADHD is a very sensitive manner. It is not just something that you can jump right into. People must have an advanced knowledge of the subject when they are treating people with ADHD or when they have ADHD themselves. Otherwise, they could end up making the problems even worse.

About The Author

Terence Williams has studied the occurrence of ADHD and has cited that neurobehavioral professionals recognize three different types of attention deficit hyperactivity disorder. The Predominant Inattentive type demonstrates as difficulties performing tasks, paying attention, organizing tasks and following directions. The person may forget details of performing tasks or may become distracted from the task at hand.

The Predominantly Hyperactive or Impulsive type has difficulty sitting still, may run around constantly, and find many outlets for physical activity rather than sit in one place. The person may also interrupt people in conversation, grab things away from people at inappropriate times or speak out of turn. The impulsivity can demonstrate as frequent accidents or injuries. The Combined type of ADHD can show all of these symptoms in approximately equal amounts.

Terence has been married for nine years to a wife that suffers from ADHD and it is his self-taught expertise that has allowed him to have a long and healthy relationship. You should pick up a copy of his book The Effect ADHD Has on Marriage to gain more insights into how you can save your marriage and how to recognize the signs in your spouse.

Adult ADHD Treatment: The Pros And Cons

How To Treat ADHD Effectively

Ashley Bell

ADULT ADHD TREATMENT: THE PROS AND CONS

HOW TO TREAT ADHD EFFECTIVELY

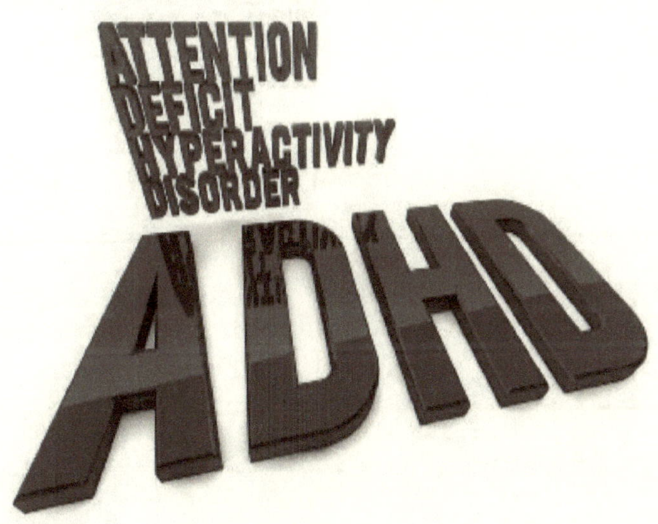

ASHLEY BELL

About The Author

Ashley Bell has always been interested in the way that certain diseases affect individuals. One of her interests is adult ADHD as there are members in her family that suffer from that condition. She found that she had to read quite a number of texts just to get the information to she wanted. After thinking about what she had to go through, she made the decision to put together a text that would have all the information that anyone could need in one simple text.

The aim that Ashley has is to ensure that anyone seeking information on ADHD in adults will have no challenges finding the information that they want. Contrary to what many believe, it is not a condition that is to be taken lightly as the effects that this condition can have on an individual are extremely detrimental to their overall wellbeing.

Chapter 1 What Is Adult ADHD?

Adult Attention Deficit Hyperactivity Disorder (ADHD) is a condition found in 60 percent of adults who suffered with ADHD as a child. ADHD is a complex neurological and behavioral condition that results in problems such as inattention, erratic and impulsive behavior and inability to complete tasks. Patients with ADHD are frequently quick tempered, impatient and have poor or non-existent organizational skills.

The onset of ADHD is exclusively in childhood. The condition does not develop in adults. Adults with ADHD may not have been diagnosed with the disorder in childhood and investigation into his or her past may help confirm a diagnosis. A history of poor performance in school and multiple disciplinary actions may point to ADHD. Often children with ADHD have to repeat one or more grade levels in school and have a higher overall dropout rate. Interviewing the adult patient's parents, if possible, is an excellent way to gather evidence to support an ADHD diagnosis.

Symptoms in Adults with ADHD can be mild, allowing the patient to effectively cope and work around issues such as the inability to concentrate. Patients with a mild form of the disease may have a difficult time accomplishing mundane tasks, but have no problem staying focused on activities of great interest to them. Patients displaying mild symptoms may be able to easily use coping mechanisms to control impulses. For instance, an individual may be able to establish a habit of deep breathing and counting to 15 when an impulse of anger or frustration begins to surface.

Adults living with more severe cases of ADHD have a much more difficult time coping with symptoms on their own. Concentrating and completing tasks will remain difficult no matter how interesting or exciting the activity. Often frustration leads to destructive behavior and poor or nonexistent relationships.

Adults suffering from the condition often have a difficult time maintaining personal relationships. Patients with ADHD often have a high divorce rate and go through multiple marriages. Frequent problems occur in the patient's relationships due to an inability to control impulses and angry outbursts. Difficulties in task completion may cause disruptions in relationships leading to further discord.

Job stability and performance is another area that adults living with ADHD have problems with. The inability to remember assignments often results in missed meetings and deadlines. Tasks at work are often not able to be completed as the adult moves from one task to another without finishing the first assignment. Organizational skills are poor or not present in patients with ADHD resulting in slow and poor job performance. Uncontrolled outbursts of anger matched with a low threshold for frustration and impatience can cause problems with other employees. Sufferers from ADHD typically move frequently from job to job, have insufficient work skills and a poor employment history.

Multiple social problems often plague the adult patient that suffers with ADHD as well. The inability to succeed at work and keep a job often keeps the individual at a lower socioeconomic status. Difficulties in controlling temper and having higher levels of impatience and a decreased threshold for frustration is often negatively displayed on the road. It is not uncommon for adults with ADHD to have multiple traffic violations resulting in tickets, suspensions and accidents. Problems with driving compounds the individual's problems by making it difficult to get to work due to suspensions and increased debt due to court fees and elevated insurance costs.

Social maladjustment in the adult with ADHD often leads to substance abuse. Patients are more likely to smoke cigarettes and look for ways to alleviate emotional discomfort through substance abuse. Alcohol abuse and illegal drug use are common ways that ADHD patients use to escape from the emotional pains caused by their affliction. Becoming impaired often allows ADHD patients to feel more comfortable in social situations by giving them a false sense of confidence.

Treatments in ADHD employ pharmaceutical prescriptions, behavior modification or a combination of the two. Several medications are available by prescriptions that are effective in treating the symptoms of ADHD. Interestingly, though hyperactivity is a component of the disorder, stimulants are used to treat the malady and produce a calming effect. Even though stimulants work well in controlling the symptoms of ADHD, the nature of the condition makes drug use a sometimes precarious choice. ADHD patients are often prone to substance abuse and stimulants are controlled substances that are often abused illegally. A tendency to be forgetful and a lack of organization in the patient with ADHD often lead to over medicating or under dosing.

Effective behavioral treatments are also employed in adults with ADHD. Goals for impulse and anger control along with routines to help with concentration and organization are implemented incrementally. New techniques and habits need to be introduced slowly to individuals with ADHD in order to avoid the onset of frustration. New habits that are introduced individually are more likely to be mastered and established. Psychological therapy is also started to help the patient view themselves more positively and establish confidence. A higher self esteem will result in confidence enabling the patient to foster positive relationships and take pride in work and other accomplishments.

Patients undergoing treatment for ADHD should be frequently monitored on their progress. Improvements and changes in symptoms will call for treatment modifications and goal changes. With proper diagnosis, individuals with ADHD can relieve their suffering and move toward leading healthier lives with more positive relationships and personal success.

Chapter 2 What Are the Three Types of Adult ADHD?

There are three types of Attention Deficit Hyperactivity Disorder that affect adults: Predominantly hyperactive-impulse, predominantly inattentive, and a combined form of the two (hyperactivity impulse and inattentiveness). Without treatment, the symptoms can be devastating to the adult, both socially and professionally.

Hyperactivity-impulse in adults often shows up as being fidgety; pacing while on the phone, jiggling their legs and not being able to stay seated are all classic hyperactivity-impulse symptoms. Losing items needed for daily living, such as car keys, cell phones, and glasses, being unable to focus on tasks, and not listening are all indicators of inattentiveness.

The combined form of hyperactivity-impulse and inattentive disorder is the most destructive of the ADHD disorders. Consider this: An employee who jiggles their leg may be distracting or even annoying to other workers, but this behavior alone is not destructive to the job environment. But an employee who jiggles their leg, losses important documents and interrupts others will probably experience a long line of short-term employment. This can be financially devastating to a person.

A person exhibiting multiple symptoms of combined ADHD will most likely have trouble staying in committed relationships due to an inability to concentrate on what the other person is saying or to listen fully when the other person speaks. Combine that with a constant need to interrupt the significant other and the results will be disastrous on a relationship.

In predominantly hyperactivity-impulse ADHD, the symptoms may include one or more of the following and can range from mild to severe: Squirming, fidgeting, interrupting others, talking excessively, and having difficulty remaining seated. Sometimes they are unable to wait in line or to wait their turn. They will leave lines at the drive through windows or grocery stores in frustration.

In predominantly inattentive ADHD the symptoms may include: Being distracted, making careless mistakes, losing important items such as glasses or car keys, not paying attention, not paying attention to details, not staying focused on a task, not listening, avoiding involved or detailed tasks, and not being able to follow instructions. With this type of ADHD, a person will often be late for meetings or work due to being distracted. However, they may 'hyperfocus' on a project and forget important things, such as picking up a child at school or taking a baking cake out of the oven. This type of ADHD can cause a person to be unable to control their thoughts, making them appear flighty and unfocused. Often, to cover up for this inability, they will fake an understanding only to be exposed when they are questioned about a conversation or set of instructions.

In the combined form of ADHD symptoms will include characteristics of both hyperactivity-impulsivity and inattentive types. These symptoms have to be exhibited for more than six months and be a hindrance to daily living to be diagnosed as ADHD types. Usually the symptoms will have showed up before age seven, but they may not be recognized or diagnosed until the adolescent or adult years. Proper early diagnosis is critical to the health and well-being of the individual. Great damage can be done to the psyche of an un-diagnosed person who is unable to maintain a job or relationship with others.

The cause of ADHD is unknown but research suggests three different reasons for the development of ADHD which are biological-base, toxins or genetics. In biological based thinking, it is believed that there is a lower metabolic activity in the brain in areas controlling judgment, attention and movement. In the toxin-based theory it is believed that environmental toxins such as alcohol, drugs or even red dyes in food and drinks can cause ADHD. In genetic-based thinking it is believed that genes such as the dopamine neurotransmitter are linked to the problem, or that the disease 'runs in the family'. None of these ideas have been conclusively proven.

The treatment of ADHD in all of the types varies from medications and behavioral therapy to alternative treatments such as special colored glasses and chiropractic adjustments. Medications, usually stimulants such as Ritalin, Dexedrine and Adderall are common treatment of ADHD. Stimulants are used to increase the activity of under-active parts of the brain in those with ADHD. However, stimulants are linked to weight loss, sleeplessness and decreased appetite. Some are also believed to cause suicidal thoughts.

Behavioral therapy includes positive reinforcement with rewards for improved behavior. It is very important to have clear communications and that the employer or significant other is willing to be patient while therapy is being performed.

Alternative treatments, while not recognized by the medical community, often have good results. Biofeedback, allergy treatments and special diets are some alternatives to medication. It is important to remember that different treatments work better on different patients and what works for one person may be ineffective or have adverse side-effects on another person.

When treating ADHD it is important to communicate with your care provider about the effectiveness or lack thereof of treatment options. Inform them of any side effects noted immediately, especially suicidal thoughts or depression. Also let them know of any improvements from the treatment. Communication is essential to adjusting the treatments and optimizing the results for individuals.

With the treatment options available today, it is not only possible but probable that an option can be designed which will allow individuals with any of the forms of ADHD to live productive lives.

Chapter 3 How Can Adult ADHD Be Treated

The treatment for ADHD usually needs to be a multi-pronged approach of medication, therapy, and oftentimes family therapy. The type of medication and therapy that is used will vary depending on each patient's specific needs, family background, and history of treatment. Since ADHD has shown a genetic link in families, even the patient's family history of treatment needs to be assessed to determine what successful measures have been taken in the past.

When the time comes to determine which type of medication is right for a patient, the type is usually determined based on any other health concerns the patient might already have. Many of the medications used to treat ADHD are stimulants such as Ritalin, Focalin, Vyvanse, Adderall, Concerta, and Quillivant. Most of these medications are also used to treat children, however when it comes to adult patients other factors may determine whether a stimulant is the right approach to treatment.

If the patient has a history of substance abuse, often times something other than a stimulant will be prescribed due to the propensity of abuse for stimulants in adults. In these instances Strattera or Wellbutrin, which work slower than stimulants, can be prescribed to the patient.

While medications generally help with the symptoms of ADHD, some form of therapy is needed to help the patient with their day to day functions. For example if a patient can't remember to take their medication, due to the forgetfulness associated with ADHD, adhering to multiple dosing throughout the day will be difficult. This is where some form of Cognitive Behavior Therapy or Life Coaching becomes beneficial to the patient.

Cognitive Behavior Therapy teaches the patient how to have a more positive structured life. The patient learns how to change negative thinking patterns into positive ones. More often than not individuals with ADHD hear how lazy they are from others or that they can't do anything right, they begin to internalize these thoughts which leads to the creation of a negative self image.

Many times it is the depression and anxiety associated with this thought process that forces the individual to seek help without knowing they have ADHD; as many as 80% of patients suffer from co-occurring disorders such as anxiety and depression. Once the patients thought process is changed they can focus on learning how to become more organized and focused. The therapy can help them develop better problem solving skills and how to control impulsive behavior.

Cognitive Behavior Therapy can be either in an individual or group setting. One of the biggest advantages of a group setting offers the patient a chance to meet others with ADHD allowing them to draw from others experiences. Individuals in a group setting can draw from similar experiences, share information, and discuss techniques they have used to solve problems. One of the biggest downsides for group therapy is that some individuals may not feel comfortable sharing in a group setting leading to a lack of participation. Individuals who refuse to participate in a group setting are not getting the benefit of therapy and may be better suited for individual therapy sessions.

Through a Life Coach a patient can develop skills to manage the day to day functions of life. They may gain knowledge on how to use a calendar for day to day planning, how to minimize distractions throughout their day, or to find constructive outlets for excessive energy. While these might seem like simple tasks, for an individual with ADHD simply learning these three things can have a significant impact on their life. Using a calendar or making a list of things to do can help a person remember an appointment or activity they need to do. Realizing that certain things distract you throughout the day such as a loud TV or music can help an individual become more productive by simply putting in earplugs or some other method of blocking out the noise. Even developing a hobby to deal with excessive energy can have a positive impact on an individual's life instead of leading them to get involved in something that can have negative consequences.

For individuals with ADHD who have families, family therapy is often a good additional component to add to their treatment. Most family members do not understand their loved ones condition. They only see the disorganization in their life and the chaos that ensues from it. Family therapy educates other members of the family about what ADHD is and how it affects everyone involved. It provides an outlet for family members to learn how to cope with the stress of living with someone who has ADHD. Family members learn what they can do to help their loved one. They learn how to improve communication and the solving problem skills of their family unit. Considering the divorce rate for those with ADHD is very high, family therapy can promote the family staying together and working as a team.

Since ADHD affects so many areas of an individual's life, there is no one best treatment method. The treatment needs to be based on not only the individual with ADHD, but also their particular life circumstances. The treatment must also include recognizing and treating any other co-occurring disorders that exist. With so many things to consider, treating ADHD may seem like a daunting task but it is not impossible. For the patient with ADHD it is well worth it as they can have significant improvement in how they function from one day to the next.

Chapter 4 The Pros and Cons of Treating ADHD with Medication

Many options are available for the treatment of attention deficit hyperactivity disorder (ADHD). Some doctors choose to use behavioral therapy while others choose different methods of therapy. However, one of the most common treatments for this disorder is medication. A doctor may prescribe a stimulant such as Ritalin, a non-stimulant such as Strattera, an antidepressant, or an antihypertensive medication. The purpose of these medications is to manage the symptoms of ADHD. Using this course of treatment has positive and negative aspects. The following is a list of pros and cons of treating ADHD with medication:

Pros

Quick Results: If the doctor selects a dosage and medication type that works for the client and calms the symptoms, the individual may show progress very quickly. Medications typically work their way into a person's system in approximately three days. Some substances may take up to two to three weeks to provide their full effects. However, even this period is shorter than the time it would take to successfully develop a therapy strategy.

Higher Self Esteem: Many people with ADHD have low self-esteem. This may be due to the ridicule of other people or the frustration of the sufferers. Taking the medication may allow the individual to focus better or have less fits of rage and excitability. In other words, the medication may stabilize the sufferer. Emotional and mental stabilization always brings forth positive feelings. Therefore, a person who takes medicine for ADHD may start to feel better about himself or herself within the first month.

More Functionality: ADHD medications that manage the symptoms of the disorder give some clients abilities that they did not have before. The ability to concentrate on a specific task is one thing that one might gain from medication. Having a greater sense of focus and concentration can help a person to produce more at work and achieve higher grades in school. Artists and people who are involved in crafts and building can earn more money by taking medicine.

Stronger Personal Relationships: Mental illnesses are famous for causing stress in relationships. This includes parent-child relationships, friendships, co-worker relationships, romantic partnerships, and the like. Managing the symptoms that cause the stress with medication can give the sufferer a chance to gain clarity on the illness. He or she can then explain such an illness to family members and friends, which will bring them closer. Behaving in a respectable fashion will also strengthen these relationships.

Cons

Dependence: One of the worst negative aspects of treating ADHD with medication is developing a physical dependence on the medication. All psychiatric medications have some sort of dependency risk associated with them. Ritalin, which is one of the most widely used medicinal treatments for ADHD, has many unfavorable withdrawal symptoms. Such withdrawal symptoms include depression, anxiety, fatigue and cardiovascular problems. Antidepressants may also cause severe depression if the client stops taking them. Some people may have to take medications indefinitely, or wean off them slowly to avoid the aforementioned problems.

Financial Strain: ADHD medications are expensive. The average antidepressant costs approximately $150 for a 30-day supply. Ritalin costs approximately $200, and some other medications cost as much as a mortgage payment. The stress on the wallet is much less when a person has health insurance. However, the cost can be devastating for a person with no insurance who needs the medication to manage his or her symptoms.

Side Effects: Another negative aspect of treating ADHD with medication is the side effects. Many medications cause uncomfortable side effects that may or may not cause the client to stop taking it. Some of the most common side effects of ADHD medications are headaches, nausea, vomiting, brain zaps, fatigue, uneven heartbeats, dizziness, bruising, high blood pressure, blurred vision, irritability, depression, numbness, restless leg syndrome, and rashes. For some clients, the side effects subside after a number of weeks. For others, either the side effects do not cease or they worsen over time. The side effects are the number one reason that some people discontinue their medications. A person who is not medicating the condition may be agitated, flighty and aggressive.

Abuse: Unfortunately, some people choose to abuse their medication. Products such as Ritalin may provide the user with a high that was not felt before. Instead of taking the medication as prescribed, this person may take too much of it or even share it with friends or sell it. This is not the case in most situations however, parents, doctors, and clients must work together to monitor the person who is taking the medication. Any changes in behaviors or disappearance of prescriptions should set off a red flag that maybe the doctor should prescribe something different.

Making the Decision to Treat ADHD with Medication

Making the decision to treat ADHD with medication is not an easy task for anyone. Before deciding on the medicinal course of action, one should have a complete physical and a long discussion with the doctor. The individual should listen closely to the medical professional's opinions, but hold as much weight with his or her own. Additionally, the person must consider other factors such as addiction potential, health risks, and finances. If taking the medication provides more advantages than disadvantages then the right choice is to try it. However, if the client is too young or has other health problems, perhaps the individual should consider a different course of action. Therapy is always available for ADHD management.

Chapter 5 The Pros and Cons of Cognitive Behavior Treatment for ADHD

Recent studies have suggested that cognitive behavioral therapy (CBT) is often the most highly effective form of treatment available for most who suffer from ADHD. Some even suggest it can be as effective as prescription drugs.

Once a diagnosis of ADHD is made, treatment usually includes behavioral modification. Cognitive therapy suggests that the way you think affects how you behave. This form of treatment involves examining the validity of the thoughts with the main goal being to increase the frequency of appropriate actions and decrease the frequency and severity of inappropriate conduct.

It is important, however, to tailor a treatment plan to address the specific needs of a given patient. Often, a combination of therapies is required to maximize treatment effectiveness. For two reasons, among others, medication and behavioral therapy are the bedrocks of the most effective treatment programs for ADHD.

First, when coexisting conditions are present, both need to be addressed. ADHD in both children and adults is typically associated with a parallel mental disorder. Often, depression, anxiety, defiance and other relationship and learning problems are also present. It is generally agreed that in such cases, it is important to understand the importance of psychotherapeutic medications such as antidepressants or anti-anxiety medicines combined with behavioral therapy.

Second, the age of the patient is often a factor. Children who are extremely impulsive and can't cope with thinking through a situation before they react may find the therapy quite difficult.

A continuum of care that is tailored to the specific needs of the patient and addresses all aspects of that person's life, are often crucial to success. That said, the pros and cons of CBT tend to be universal for people with coexisting conditions regardless of age.

Advantages of CBT

Skills learned during CBT are useful, practical and helpful strategies to help anyone learn how to better deal with any life situation that leads to stress.

CBT can be completed in a relatively short period of time compared with other types of psychoanalytic therapies.

Because CBT involves a highly structured treatment plan it can be provided in different formats from individual to group therapy to self-help books and computer programs.

Many people cannot afford or don't want to go to ongoing therapy which can require a commitment of six months or longer. They may find it more practical and useful to focus on the more directive skills a time-limited CBT treatment can provide.

CBT is a form of treatment that has been well-researched and proven over time. As such, highly trained therapists can be found in abundance.

CBT does not carry the risk of adverse side effects sometimes associated with prescription medications that alter brain function.

From a very real standpoint, there is little risk involved in applying CBT techniques to the treatment of ADHD. Any attempt to take a step back and examine how what a person thinks affects how they behave can be beneficial. That said, CBT does have some potential drawbacks.

Disadvantages of CBT

While CBT can effectively help many people, like all treatment approaches, its success is not guaranteed. There are no easy "one size fits all" answers to the successful treatment of ADHD.

For CBT to work, a committed approach is required, and it may not be suitable for everyone. Often, a lack of follow-through on the part of the patient limits the effectiveness of CBT. Studies have shown, for instance, that the benefits derived from a CBT program directly correlate with the number of weekly home exercises completed by the participant. As is the case when learning any new skill, repetition is required.

Due to the structured nature of CBT, it may not be suitable for people with more complex coexistent mental health issues.

Some critics argue that because CBT only addresses current problems and focuses on specific issues, it does not address the possible underlying causes of mental health conditions. CBT focuses on the individual's capacity to change themselves, and it does not take into account systemic problems that often have a significant impact on an individual's health and well being.

Many complain that the CBT approach is actually harmful because their deeper emotions are easily dismissed. For them, CBT's shallow focus on the power of positive thinking and behavior modification minimize the importance of the personal condition they feel is at the root of their problem.

It is not uncommon for patients to feel that they simply don't get the results they had hoped for with CBT and to decide that, while psychodynamic therapy requires a greater investment in time and money, it is more effective for them.

It is widely acknowledged among experts that ADHD has a strong genetic component. The fact that it has an identifiable hereditary component is proof. In addition, it has been observed that the genes controlling the levels of certain brain chemicals (neurotransmitters) seem to be different in those with ADHD.

Medication and behavioral therapy are widely seen by experts as the foundation of the most effective treatment program for ADHD. At the same time, skills obtained through CBT are useful, practical and helpful strategies that can be applied to help a person better manage the stresses and difficulties associated with ADHD.

The bottom line seems to be that CBT, either alone or in conjunction with medicines that alter brain function, can be a highly effective form of treatment available for most who suffer from ADHD.

Chapter 6 Does Talk Therapy Help Treat Adult ADHD

Attention deficit hyperactivity disorder (ADHD) is often discovered in the childhood years. Then as the child gets older they can still have a lot of the symptoms as a teenager or even an adult. Adults who happen to have ADHD have a harder time than other adults. It affects their work life and their life at home. They are a lot more distracted than others so it's hard for them to concentrate.

The biggest concern about adults with ADHD is when they are driving. They are more than likely going to be more distracted which can causes them to get in a wreck or speed more often. If they keep up activities such as speeding or getting in wrecks, not only are they going to get a ticket or in trouble, they are going to more than likely get their driver's license taken away from them which can then cause a lot more problems for them pursuing their everyday activities.

Adults with ADHD may have a lot of problems with their work life. With that said, they are more like to be distracted there too. They could often be late to work, have a hard time concentrating at the task on hand, or not able to concentrate in meetings. This could get them in trouble at work or possibly even terminated. It's definitely going to be a lot harder for them to work at fast moving environments such as a fast food joints.

So the main question we ask ourselves is what adults with ADHD can do to get some extra help? Besides medication to help keep their mind at ease so they can pay attention, studies found that talk therapy can actually help treat adults with ADHD.

Talk therapy will help adults with ADHD figure out how they are feeling and what their thought process is. They need to have some positive thoughts to keep them from feeling depressed because of their ADHD. This is great since having ADHD has such a huge impact on their everyday lives. ADHD can cause adults to fight or struggle with not only depression but also with anxiety and OCD (obsessive compulsive disorder). So with talk therapy, they are going to try to help cope with these issues and help the adults who have ADHD overcome these obstacles in their lives.

Talk therapy can be done through a counselor or a psychologist. It is a counseling session that gets the adults with ADHD to talk more about their feelings. They find that just by talking about how they feel or with what's going on in your mind is like releasing the negative. If someone is to hold all those bad thoughts or feelings inside without talking about them, it is going to make them feel worse or worry about things more. By helping these adults understand why they are feeling they way they are, the counselor or psychologist can actually help them turn their thoughts around to a more positive way of thinking. On top of that, the adults with ADHD are going to continue to take their medication which in turn will help them be able to focus more.

Adults with ADHD are known to be able to focus more when they are doing something they love. So with talk therapy they are going to constantly find out what it is that makes the person focus by figuring out that love. With some, that could be anything from collecting things, playing video games, working with their hands, couponing, favorite hobbies, etc. They try to advise that if the adult can remember what they are feeling when they are doing something they love and try to have them apply how they feel with doing something they don't particularly care about. This is going to try to help them understand how to focus more with everything if at all possible. That way everyday life will become easier for those adults with ADHD.

Talk therapy is definitely a step to helping those adults. It may not be the answer for every single one of them, for we are all different and have different feelings. It definitely couldn't hurt to try though and see if talking about those feelings one is experiencing could help turn it into a more positive attribute.

The talk therapy treatments are not a super long process. They usually break it up into different sessions. That could mean some adults with ADHD may only have 6 sessions where as other may take up to 24 sessions. This will be determined by the counselor or psychologist depending on how well the adult is handling the process and if it is working for them. There are different approaches and types of therapy one can pursue. So with just a little bit of research or by asking one that you found, they will be able to help that adult with ADHD to see what is going to work best for them in their life scenario.

So to answer the question, does talk therapy help treat adult ADHD? The answer would have to be yes for most it is going to be a big help to change someone's life. The very few others that it may not work for, will still have the medication that will help get them through their everyday life and regain focus in the areas they need it.

Chapter 7 How Neurofeedback Helps Treat Adult ADHD?

Great strides have been made with the use of neurofeedback in treating ADHD. The results have been very positive. Medications help to some degree, but very significant improvements are being made using neurofeedback.

Every year parents from all over the world are seeking out alternative methods of treating ADHD in their kids. It is only logical that adults could benefit from neurofeedback as well. ADHD is a disorder that will last throughout a lifetime. It affects 1 out of every 20 adults. It is commonly detected in children by poor school performance or strange behaviors, but in adults it can disrupt social relationships and job performance.

Most adults with ADHD will experience disorder in their thoughts. They will have multiple trains of thought which seem to happen simultaneously, in rapid succession, bouncing back and forth between subjects. Outsiders see this as an inability to remain focused on topics or conversations. Adults with ADHD will exhibit abnormal emotional reactions when exposed to punishment situations, and they lack mental flexibility.

ADHD in adults shares high co morbidity with -

• Depression

• Alcohol & Drug Abuse

• Anti-social Personality Disorder

and even the tendency to smoke has been found to be more prevalent among people who have ADHD, than among those who don't.

Because ADHD is involved with self-regulatory systems, neurofeedback training is effective as a conditioning technique. It improves cognitive and psycho physiological functions. There have been numerous studies done using neurofeedback training with children, to assess the efficacy of neurofeedback for adults.

In one such study there were 142 adults, who ranged in age from 19 to 79 years, who participated in the study. Nearly half of these participants were women. During the test none of the participants were on any antidepressant medications or stimulants. The results were quite significant overall. When individual data was observed, the results were even more dramatic. The majority of the participants improved greatly with many improving above and beyond normal ranges for most individuals.

It showed that a systematic tendency for improvement in the area of attention. The most significant of these improvements occurred where pre-test scores held the most severe deficits. The results showed that neurofeedback training produced significant clinical improvement in 83% of all participants of the test. This result is superior to the already established 70% response rate to psycho stimulants.

The participants improved in the areas of impulsivity, variability, and inattention, after participating in 20 or more sessions involving neurofeedback. The effectiveness is seems all the more impressive considering that most of the participants were difficult patients who previously underwent many prior treatments with little to no success. Some of these adults had suffered from cognitive and attention disorders for as long as 20 to 30 years.

This extraordinary success rate from neurofeedback in regard to attention problems, at higher rates than the stimulant medications, implies that very profound effects on the neurobiologial mechanisms could be responsible for such good results.

Testing

Neurofeedback therapy involves providing real-time feedback for specific brain-waves. It is a conditioning method that encourages, or discourages, the brain to produce very specific frequencies. It can lead to both a permanent and a sustained effect.

Participants who undergo treatment will first need to be assessed extensively on brain function. This would be in the form of QEEG and Neuropsychological assessments. All the results are then put into a comprehensive report, which is then used to form a personalized treatment plan.

During the neurofeedback training, the participant will have electrodes placed on their scalp, while sitting opposite a computer screen. They are then instructed to use brain activity to influence activities appearing on the screen. The activity can be represented to them in numerous ways. It could simply be in the form of a solid bar graphic, or presented as a game or movie. By repeating this conditioning process, the participant begins to learn how to gain control over specific brain frequencies. This diminishes ADHD symptoms over time.

Importance of Diagnosis

Identifying ADHD in adults and equipping them with the appropriate management skills for their personal, social, and educational development, significantly improves their chances of success in life. Effective treatment improves work performance, educational achievement, and self-esteem.

The proper diagnosis of adult ADHD helps them to put their problems into the proper perspective. As adults, they usually have already developed negative self-perceptions and low self-esteem, which is the result of many social, academic, and vocational failures. Society labels them as 'slow learners', 'lazy', 'self-centered', 'spacey', 'lacking motivation', or 'having a bad attitude'.

Post-Diagnosis

Treatment methods that are supported by the professionals include education and counseling. The adult and his/her family, along with their close friends, all need to be educated about the situation and coping with it properly. There are educational and employment accommodations that may be necessary. Proper treatment depends on the severity of the person's disorder as well as the number and type of any associated problems.

A lot of adults with ADHD have seen great benefits from treatment plans that include education, counseling, and neurofeedback. It gives them a foundation to build upon for new successes. Aside from the fact that medications are costly, neurofeedback has this benefit - it can lead to permanent improvements in functionality by utilizing learned changes in brain activities.

The Brainquiry equipment used to measure the brain activity is available for home use. The active electrodes send data to a home PC or laptop, or even remotely to a PDA using Bluetooth. Neurofeedback for adult ADHD is a great advancement in today's technological age.

ADHD In Adults: Am I ADHD? Interactive Questions For ADHD Assessment

Learn If You Suffer From ADHD - Take This Assessment Test

By: Jason Newman

ABOUT THE AUTHOR

Jason Newman grew up in a household that had individuals suffering from attention deficit hyperactivity disorder and as such developed a keen interest from an early age in ADHD/ADD . This persistence interest lead him to do intense research on the topic to fine workable processes that would help parents, caregivers and friends of an individual with ADHD/ADD manage their daily lives . In college he studied psychology and also behavioral therapy and memory improvement among other courses . From the knowledge that he gained from his research and courses he was able to write a number of books on the subject

He has stated that the research that he has done has made him better able to assist his sibling; who was diagnosed with ADHD and also help him recognize ADHD/ADD traits in others . Jason experience with ADHD/ADD as allowed him to assist individuals with ADHD get the necessary treatment that they need . His work on memory improvement has also helped these individuals organize their daily activities so that they are able to function with effortlessness .

Jason is aware that individuals who believe that they have ADHD/ADD find it a demanding thing to deal with and as such explains things as best as possible in this book and his advice can help both individuals diagnosed with ADHD/ADD as well as persons that have to deal with individuals diagnosed on a daily basis .

UNDERSTANDING ADHD (ATTENTION DEFICIT HYPERACTIVITY DISORDER) ADHD or ADD (Attention Deficit Disorder) is a psychiatric disorder seen mainly in children with symptoms sometimes continuing to adulthood .

ADHD comes with restlessness, impulsive action and impaired ability to learn due to lack of concentration . Symptoms of ADHD appear before seven years of age, and impact the school-aged children most . ADHD affects about 3 to 5 percent children globally, and seen more frequently in boys as compared to girls . ADHD is a chronic disorder, with most individuals diagnosed in childhood continuing to have symptoms to adulthood . ADHD in children can be confused with similar conditions like Asperger's Syndrome and Autism, where there is lacking social interaction, expression and symptoms of hyperactivity .

ADHD or similar diseases does not affect the physical growth, e . g . weight, height or does not cause any physical deformity . SIGNS AND SYMPTOMS OF ADHD Initial ADHD symptoms in childhood can appear with slow learning, hyperactivity, lack of attention, impulsive and disruptive behavior . With progressing age after childhood, symptoms of ADHD vary in different stages of life with a slow "improvement" in the learning skills .

Adults can also have signs of ADHD; as a matter of fact, studies have shown that half the adults; who have been diagnosed with ADHD had carried the symptoms from their childhood into their adulthood, but symptoms of ADHD usually changes as the person enters into adulthood . For instance, instead of hyperactivity; present in childhood, the same person may well experience some degree of restlessness as an adult . Adults with symptoms of ADHD, in addition may have interpersonal relationship problems which might include trouble at work .

ADHD IN ADULTS Adults suffering with ADHD may have difficulty remembering information, following directions, organizing tasks, concentrating, or completing work within given time . If such difficulties are not managed appropriately, there can be associated vocational, emotional, behavioral, social and academic problems . Statistics of Adult ADHD: • ADHD affects males more than females in childhood, but this ratio seems to become even by adulthood .

• ADHD affects approximately 3 to 10 percent of school-aged children .

An estimated 60 percent amongst them will continue having symptoms to adulthood . Common problems faced by Adult with ADHD The following problems may arise from ADHD: • Impulsiveness • Difficulty controlling anger • Anxiety and depression • Chronic boredom • Chronic lateness and forgetfulness • Employment problems • Difficulty concentrating when reading • Low frustration tolerance • Mood swings • Low self-esteem • Procrastination (postpone work) • Relationship problems, lack of social interaction • Poor organization skills • Substance abuse or addiction During schooling, adults with ADHD may have underperformed, faced frequent school disciplinary actions, had to repeat a grade or have often dropped from school .

SOCIAL IMPAIRMENTS LINKED TO ADULT ADHD ADHD adults with are more likely to: • Self-report psychological maladjustment • Have a lower socioeconomic status • Violate driving rules • Smoke cigarettes, or use illegal substances more frequently ADHD VERSUS NORMAL ADHD symptoms are not very uncommon, and sometimes many 'normal' people experience symptoms similar to ADHD .

A normal person at certain times can also be impulsive, hyperactive or can face lack of concentration, but if the symptoms are present continuously that is affecting the daily functioning, it is a condition of ADHD . Quite often bad or some shocking experience in the past of a normal person can affect the present and future, but ADHD is not the cause for such developments . As mood or anxiety disorders also present themselves with similar symptoms as ADHD, it gets difficult to diagnose ADHD in adults . In contrast to normal people, adults with ADHD might face more marital problems (or multiple marriages), and can have higher incidence of separation or divorce . Much of the impairment associated with ADHD diminishes with time, and remission of the disorder can be mitigated with appropriate treatment .

FACTS ABOUT ADHD There is no concrete evidence that can list the exact cause (or causes) that gives rise to such disorder, but there are certain facts that provide indications on its occurrence .

Hereditary traits - ADHD can be a family illness or symptoms can present in genealogy . Altered brain anatomy and function - Brain scanning of people with ADHD shows difference in activity and certain structures of the brain . For example, an ADHD person might not have as much activity in the part of the brain that controls attention, as compared to a normal person . Exposure to toxins - Pregnant females who have used drugs, smoke or taken alcohol or exposed to environmental poisons like PCBs (polychlorinated biphenyls) are at higher risk of giving birth to ADHD offspring(s) . Exposure to lead (found in paint) is often linked to cause change in behavior .

ADHD does not lead to any other developmental or psychological conditions; for example, it does not affect the physical growth or appearance of the person . The height, weight and other physical characteristics are absolutely natural, and ADHD in a person cannot be ascertained just by looking at the person .

DISORDERS ASSOCIATED WITH ADHD Disorders in mood - Mood disorders like bipolar disorder and depression can often be seen in people with ADHD . Disorders with anxiety - Anxiety disorders including nervousness and excess worry occur frequently in adults that have ADHD . Such disorder worsens with the setbacks and challenges faced by person with

ADHD .

Personality disorders - Adults having ADHD have a higher risk of getting personality disorders like borderline personality disorder and antisocial personality disorder .

WHAT CAN BE DONE? A person suffering from ADHD can also cause disturbances in the lives of people associated with him or her .

It is quite likely that an ADHD person will not approach a doctor, psychiatrist or psychologist to get self-treatment, but these health personnel might be approached by people who are associated with the person suffering from ADHD . Nevertheless, if one's life is continuously disrupted by hyperactivity, impulsive behavior, hyperactivity or inattention, it is better to consult a doctor for suggestions and help .

Doctor may find out the triggering causes that worsens or alleviates the ADHD (e . g . stress, any particular diet or environment), suggest supplements, medications, or alternate treatment so that the ADHD patient can live a better life, with more peaceful social interactions with other people .

MAKING A DIAGNOSIS OF ADULT ADHD Diagnosis of ADHD in adults can be difficult because its symptoms may also be similar to other conditions . The mental health care provider attempts to diagnose ADHD in adults by ruling out other similar conditions .

CONDITIONS SIMILAR TO ADHD There can be conditions or illnesses that might have caused symptoms similar to ADHD to arise .

1 . Medications and drugs .

Drugs, alcohol or medications can cause neurological changes in brain can make a person exhibit ADHD-like symptoms .

2 . Similar mental disorders .

ADHD symptoms can resemble symptoms of other mental health issues such as psychotic disorders like mood, anxiety and adjustment disorders (unable to cope with stress), and language and learning deficits .

3 . Additional health issues .

Symptoms similar to that of ADHD can arise with developmental disorders, seizures, sleep apnea, low blood sugar, thyroid disorder, lead poisoning, and vision or hearing problems .

In such cases, the doctor usually directs the patient to the appropriate specialist or suggests adequate diagnosis for the condition .

EVALUATING CHILDHOOD ADHD SYMPTOMS Signs and symptoms of ADHD typically arise before the age of 7 that may continue to adulthood in the same or indefinable form . The doctor diagnosing ADHD in an adult would go over his or her childhood experiences, and analyze the old school records, and get information from teachers, spouse, siblings, parents and friends . DIAGNOSTIC CRITERION FOR ADHD There is no one-symptom that can explicitly distinguish a person affected with ADHD . Doctors follow the standards outlined in the DSM (Diagnostic and Statistical manual of Mental Disorders) published by the American psychiatric Association . The assessment criteria was originally intended for diagnosis of ADHD in children, but later on, the same was also followed for adults .

At least 6 of following symptoms need to be present to consider an adult of ADHD: • Hyperactivity and/or impulsiveness • Forgetfulness • Easily distracted or improper attention • Inattentiveness • Frequent mistakes • Lack of concentration or focus • Inattentiveness towards a person in direct conversation • Cannot properly or timely complete tasks • Cannot follow instructions • Cannot properly organize activities or tasks • Avoid tasks requiring substantial thought • Misplace important things • Tendency to fidget with the hands or feet, or squirm while seated • Leave room when expected to sit • Act inappropriately in certain situations • Problems doing activities silently • Seems to be full of energy, and tends to be moving all the time .

• Speaks excessively • Tendency to utter answers before a question is complete • Cannot wait patiently in relaxed manner, tends to show irritation • Tendency to interfere or interrupt in other people's conversations Besides the 6 symptoms from the above list, an individual adult with ADHD can show additional characteristics or symptoms that include: • Hyperactive, impulsive or inattentive symptoms present before the age of seven that might have caused injury in the past • Different behavior at childhood compared to other children of the same age without ADHD • Have had the symptoms for at least 6 months • Symptoms may have jeopardized relationships, life at school, home and/or work The doctor may look carefully about relationships with family and performance at school or work, and may consider other symptoms, that are best visualized by the doctor's experience .

DRUGS AND TREATMENTS There is no single treatment that can cure a person of ADHD . Treatments commonly administered include psychological counseling and/or medication . Depending upon the patient, therapy and medication are usually provided together to get the best outcome . MEDICATIONS Psycho-stimulants are the most typical medications prescribed for ADHD . These stimulant medications appear to balance and boost the neurotransmitters levels in the brain . The objectives of the medications for ADHD are mainly targeted to treat hyperactivity and inattention . The effects of the drugs can wear-off quickly if taken for a short time . In addition, the dose would vary between patients, so it may take time to find the most suitable dosage for an individual .

Some popular stimulants used to treat ADHD are: • Lisdexamfetamine (Vyvanse) • Dextroamphetamine (Dexedrine) • Dextroamphetamine-amphetamine (Adderall) • Methylphenidate (Metadate, Daytrana, Concerta, Ritalin) The effect of stimulant drugs can be either be short or long acting .

Short acting can last up to four hours, while long acting can last from 6 to 12 hours . Methylphenidate is a drug that comes in a patch (like Band-Aid or Nicotine patch), and it can be easily worn on the hip . The medication is gradually released in the body through the skin, and that lasts for about 9 hours . It can take up to 3 hours for the effect of medication to be felt, and it is not to be frequently taken (follow the advice of doctor) . Like other medications, the stimulants come with side effects . The person can observe abdominal pain, liver problems, nausea, elevated pulse, elevated blood pressure, headache, psychosis (delusions), insomnia reduced appetite (anorexia), and weight loss . In some cases, there can be tics resulting in a sudden involuntary spasmodic muscular contraction, especially of facial, neck, or shoulder muscles . For most individuals, these medicines are considered safe for treating ADHD in the long term . However, the doctor may not immediately recommend these drugs, if the individual has issues with drug or alcohol use . Sometimes, additional medications are also considered to treat ADHD: • Antidepressants like venlafaxine (Effexor) and bupropion (Wellbutrin) • Atomoxetine (Strattera) Venlafaxine or bupropion is often advised for symptoms of ADHD with mood disorder .

The effects of these medications are not as rapid as stimulants, and might take a few weeks for their effect to come . These medications are best-suited if stimulants cannot be taken due to any reason, such as any health condition, tic disorder, drug abuse or suffer with the side effects of stimulants .

Side effects of atomoxetine can include sweating, painful urination, decreased libido, slightly elevated blood pressure and heart rate, decreased appetite, nausea and insomnia .

Bupropion side effects may initially include anxiety, sweating, dry mouth, constipation, nausea, headache and insomnia; but the side effects gradually lessen as the body gets used to this medication . Very rarely, seizures can occur- the higher the dose of bupropion, the greater the risk of seizures . Bupropion has less effect on sexual libido compared to atomoxetine . Side effects of venlafaxine include rise in blood pressure (with high doses), loose bowel movements, nausea, headache and insomnia .

These side effects reduce as the body gets used to the medication . For many individuals, decrease in sexual ability or desire is a side effect of great concern that may cause hindrance in using the medication .

CLOSER LOOK AT EACH MEDICATION

What type of medication is Vyvanse? Vyvanse is a CNS (central nervous system) stimulant administered to treat Attention Deficit Hyperactivity Disorder (ADHD) . It affects the brain chemicals and nerves that contribute to impulse control and hyperactivity . Vyvanse is not given to children below 6 years . It is essentially similar to Dexedrine, which has been abused and overused as a diet pill for a long time . What type of ingredients does it contain? The drug is believed to simulate the nervous system by increasing the release or reducing the inactivation of norepinephrine and dopamine in the brain .

The nerves use these chemicals (neurotransmitters) for communication . The drug was approved by FDA in February 2007 . Comparison of Vyvanse with Adderall Adderall is 75% dextroamphetamine (dexedrine) + 25% levoamphetamine Vyvanse is 100% dextroamphetamine as the active ingredient . What are the benefits? Vyvanse is among the most effective treatment for ADHD, and the effect of Vyvanse is for much longer period of time possibly up to 12 hours .

It is prepared from the "d-type amphetamine" and not "l-type" . D-type amphetamine is considered more effective and/or has less of the side effects of the l-type (Adderall, by contrast, is a mixture of d and l-amphetamines, which means that it is more powerful, and have different or more side effects)

What type of dosage is usually recommended? The starting dose recommended is 30 mg once a day in the morning (avoid afternoon dose to prevent insomnia) . It can be taken in the morning with or without food .

Dosage may be incremented gradually with 10 mg or 20 mg at weekly intervals (maximum recommended dose = 70 mg each day) . Vyvanse capsules can be taken as whole, or empty the contents of the capsule in a glass of water, stir well until completely dispersed and consume immediately; it must not be stored .

At least one capsule must be taken a day, and single capsule must not be divided . How long can an individual take this medication? Most individuals with ADHD will need to be on medication for long term . However, the amount of the medication necessary may vary from reduced dose to increased dose, depending on the response of the patient to the medication .

ADHD is a chronic disorder and can last throughout the patient's natural life . However, some patients can be withdrawn from medication periodically if they are able to control the disorder in some other way .

What are the possible side effects of Vyvanse? Serious allergic reaction symptoms that need immediate attention by a physician: breathing difficulty, hives, swelling of the face lips, tongue or throat .

The most common side effects of Vyvanse include anxiety, loss of appetite, decreased appetite, nausea, diarrhea, trouble sleeping, dizziness, upper stomach pain, dry mouth, vomiting, irritability, weight loss and loss of sexual desire . A patient should contact their physician if he/she experiences new symptoms or worsening of above mentioned symptoms . Vyvanse can slow down the growth (height and weight) in children in long term use . Who should be closely monitored when taking Vyvanse? It is not clear whether Vyvanse will harm an unborn baby . However, the drug may pass to breast milk and may harm a nursing baby, and hence it is not advised for breastfeeding women . Growth in children and teenagers must be checked closely when on Vyvanse Sudden death in children and adolescents as been reported with patients who have serious heart problems or congenital heart defects .

Vyvanse must be avoided or very closely monitored in patients with: • high blood pressure • congenital heart defect • heart rhythm disorder, heart failure, or recent heart attack • seizure disorder or epilepsy • a personal / family history of psychotic disorder, mental illness, depression, bipolar illness, or suicide attempt • Tourette's syndrome or tics (muscle twitches) .

What in case of missed dose? Take the missed dose when you remember, but if it is close to the next scheduled dose .

Do NOT take extra dose to make up for the missed one .

What in case of overdose? Seek emergency medical attention .

Overdose symptoms may include tremor, restlessness, muscle twitches, confusion, rapid breathing, hallucinations, aggressiveness, panic, tenderness or muscle pain, muscle weakness, flu or fever symptoms, and dark colored urine .

Other overdose symptoms include vomiting, nausea, diarrhea, uneven heartbeats, stomach pain, feeling light-headed, fainting, seizure (convulsions) or coma .

Contraindications Vyvanse / lisdexamfetamine is NOT to be used in cases of: • moderate to severe high blood pressure (hypertension) • arteriosclerosis (hardening of the arteries) • heart disease • glaucoma • overactive thyroid • history of drug or alcohol addiction • severe anxiety, tension, or agitation Warnings and Precautions • Vyvanse must not be used if the person has used an MAO inhibitor such as isocarboxazid (Marplan), phenelzine (Nardil), tranylcypromine (Parnate), selegiline (Eldepryl, Emsam) or rasagiline (Azilect) or within the past 14 days .

Serious, life-threatening side effects can occur if Vyvanse is taken BEFORE the MAO inhibitor has cleared from the person's body .

• After taking Vyvanse, do not drive or operate dangerous machinery that requires alertness .

• Do not stop taking this drug without consulting your doctor .

• There can be increase in blood pressure and heart rate .

• Serious cardiovascular reactions: Avoid use in patients with known structural cardiac abnormalities, coronary artery disease, cardiomyopathy, or serious heart arrhythmia .

Reported cases of sudden death in children and with serious heart problems, as well as sudden death, stroke, and myocardial infarction in adults .

• Psychiatric adverse reactions: May cause manic or psychotic symptoms in patients with no past history, or aggravation of symptoms in patients with preexisting psychosis .

Bipolar disorder needs to be evaluated prior to stimulant use .

• Suppression of growth: Monitor weight and height in pediatric patients during treatment, as long-term use of Vyvanse can affect a child's height and weight, and slow the growth rate .

• Vyvanse is a federally controlled substance (CII), because it can lead to dependence or be abused .

DEXTROAMPHETAMINE (DEXEDRINE)

What type of medication is Dexedrine? Dexedrine is a stimulant drug used to treat (ADHD) and narcolepsy (suddenly falling asleep at inappropriate times without any control) . Stimulant medications are used to treat the symptoms of hyperactivity, impulsivity, and difficulties with focus and attention in individuals with ADHD .

Dexedrine is not given to children below 6 years . What type of ingredients does it contain? The dextroamphetamine salts constitute around 75% of the ADHD drug Adderall . Active Ingredient: dextroamphetamine sulfate What are the benefits? It controls hyperactivity, increases concentration, helps to focus on tasks- for instance taking lectures . The drug has been given to people (even USAF pilots) to help people remain focused and alert for a very long time . Types of Dexedrine pills Dexedrine pills are available in two forms: i) Short-acting: Available in 5 and 10 mg tablets, it begins working within 20 to 30 minutes of ingestion and remains effective for approximately 4 - 5 hours . ii) Long-acting pill (spansules): . Available in 5, 10 and 15 mg tablets, although it does not begin working as quickly, the sustained-release version allows the medication to remain effective for an extended period of time .

What type of dosage is usually recommended? Start with 5 mg once or twice daily; daily dosage may be increased by 5 mg/week until optimal response is obtained .

(maximum recommended dose = 40 mg each day) . It can be taken in morning (avoid afternoon dose to prevent insomnia), with or without food . Dose may vary for Narcolepsy . The medication can be interrupted occasionally to check for any recurrence of behavioral symptoms . How long can an individual take this medication? Most individuals with ADHD will need to be on medication for long term . However, the amount of the medication necessary may vary from reduced dose to increased dose, depending on the response of the patient to the medication . ADHD is a chronic disorder and can last throughout the patient's natural life .

However, some patients can be withdrawn from medication periodically if they are able to control the disorder in some other way . What are the possible side effects of Dexedrine? Serious allergic reaction symptoms that need immediate attention by a physician: breathing difficulty, hives, swelling of the face lips, tongue or throat .

The most common side effects of Dexedrine include anxiety, loss of appetite, decreased appetite, nausea, diarrhea, trouble sleeping, dizziness, upper stomach pain, dry mouth, vomiting, irritability, weight loss and loss of sexual desire .

A patient should contact physician if he/she experiences new symptoms or worsening of above mentioned symptoms .

Vyvanse can slow down the growth (height and weight) in children in long term use .

Who should be closely monitored when taking Dexedrine? Pregnancy: Can lead to premature delivery and low birth weight of infant .

Infants may experience withdrawal symptoms including agitation, dysphoria, exhaustion and weakness .

The drug passes to breast milk and may harm a nursing baby, and hence it is not advised for breastfeeding women .

Growth in children and teenagers must be checked closely when on Dexedrine .

This medication must NOT be taken with MAO inhibitors such as phenelzine or tranylcypromine .

There must be at least 14 day gap . What in case of missed dose? Take the missed dose when you remember, but if it is close to the next scheduled dose . Do NOT take extra dose to make up for the missed one (never take 2 doses at once) . What in case of overdose? Seek emergency medical attention .

Overdose symptoms may include coma, rapid breathing, confusion, tremor, fever, irregular heartbeat, hallucinations, aggressiveness, panic restlessness, muscle twitches, nausea, diarrhea or vomiting, rapid breathing .

Contraindications Do not take Dexedrine in case of: • moderate-to-severe high blood pressure • overactive thyroid gland (hyperthyroidism) • glaucoma (increased pressure in the eye) • heart disease • history of consumption of alcohol • arteriosclerosis (hardening of the arteries) • Psychomotor agitation (unintentional motions that result from mental tension and anxiety) .

Warnings and Precautions Dexedrine may be habit-forming if used for a long period of time, and hence it has a high potential for abuse and .

Abuse of Dexedrine may cause serious blood vessel problems, heart problems, or sudden death .

• Dexedrine may cause sleeplessness .

Do not take the medication near bedtime .

• After medication, take care when driving or operating heavy equipment .

• Avoid caffeinated drinks (e . g . , coffee, cocoa, tea, chocolate, cola) as it may increase the side effects of Dexedrine .

• Avoid baking soda (sodium bicarbonate) when taking dexedrine .

• Blood pressure and heart rate needs to be monitored .

• The medication is tapering off slowly over time can reduce your symptoms; if you take a low or moderate dose, you are less likely to feel withdrawal symptoms when you stop taking Dexedrine .

• Suppression of growth: Monitor weight and height in teenagers/pediatric patients during treatment .

WHAT TYPE OF MEDICATION IS ADDERALL?

Adderall is a combination of dextroamphetamine and amphetamine .

It comes in a class of medications known as central nervous system stimulant because it works by changing the amounts of certain natural chemicals in the brain .

Adderall is used to control symptoms of attention deficit hyperactivity disorder (ADHD) in children and adults, where people have difficulty focusing or controlling actions .

Adderall is also used to treat narcolepsy (person falls asleep without control) .

Adderall is not given to children below 3 years .

How does Adderall help in brain function? Adderall raises the level of dopamine and norepinephrine in the brain, thereby acting as a stimulant, which also increases the blood pressure and heart rate .

All this gives most users a feeling of alertness and an improvement in their ability to concentrate .

What are the benefits? Adderall is usually prescribed to patients who need help with the following: • Concentrate on specific tasks for long time • Remain alert during the day • Improving focus, and being less distracted • Reduce tiredness associated with narcolepsy and similar sleep disorders • Adderall has often been taken illegally by athletes for better performance .

What type of dosage is usually recommended? • In children from 3 to 5 years: Start with 2 .

5 mg daily; increase daily dosage in increments of 2 .

5 mg at weekly intervals .

• 6 years of age and older: Start with 5 mg once or twice daily; increase daily dosage in increments of 5 mg at weekly intervals • There must be interval of 4 to 6 hours between two consecutive dosages .

• It should be taken in the morning, (not in late afternoon, as it may cause difficulty falling asleep), and can be taken with or without food .

• Take capsules as whole, do not crush or chew them .

If a person cannot swallow, empty the contents on a teaspoon of applesauce and swallow immediately .

Do not divide the capsule contents in more than one dose .

What are the possible side effects of Adderall? Side effects of Adderall may vary from person-to-person .

A person may experience loss of appetite, trouble sleeping, dry mouth, fever, nervousness, dizziness, nausea, stomach pain and diarrhea .

There can be mood disorders such as mood swings, depression, aggression, and loss in changes in sexual desire (libido) .

Serious side effects includes rapid heartbeat, difficulty in breathing or swallowing, difficulty in speech (or change in voice), chest pain .

Such side effects must be immediately attended .

Who should be closely monitored when taking Adderall? • People who have any heart problem (arrhythmia, heart disease, valve problems etc) • People with overactive thyroid (hyperthyroidism) • Glaucoma (excess of fluid pressures in optic nerves) • People who are habituated to excess alcohol/drugs or other contraindicative medications • People who have seizures or mental/mood disorders (psychotic disorder, bipolar disorder, depression) • Pregnancy .

The drug can result in premature delivery of infants, who may also suffer with low birth weight . Breast-feeding is not recommended while using this drug . Consult your doctor before breast-feeding . What in case of missed dose? Take the missed dose when you remember, but if it is close to the next scheduled dose . Do NOT take extra dose to make up for the missed one (never take 2 doses at once) .

What in case of overdose? Seek emergency medical attention . Overdose symptoms may include coma, rapid breathing, confusion, tremor, fever, irregular heartbeat, hallucinations, aggressiveness, panic restlessness, muscle twitches, nausea, diarrhea or vomiting, rapid breathing, Warnings and Precautions • Adderall is addictive in nature .

Initially, when a person is new to this drug, it is very effective, but as the body adjusts to the drug gradually, more Adderall is needed for the same effect (or the effect of drug seems ineffective) .

• Adderall may be habit-forming if used for a long period of time, and hence it has a high potential for abuse .

• Abuse of Adderall may cause serious blood vessel problems, heart problems, or sudden death .

• Adderall may make cause dizziness .

Hence, driving and using dangerous machinery is not advised after consuming Adderall .

• Before any surgery, inform your doctor/dentist that you are on this medication .

• Adderall may cause sleeplessness .

Do not take the medication near bedtime .

• While on this medication, take fruit juice only after approval from doctor .

• After medication, take care when driving or operating heavy equipment .

• Limit alcoholic beverages .

Avoid caffeinated drinks (e . g . , coffee, cocoa, tea, chocolate, cola) as it may increase the side effects of Adderall .

• Blood pressure and heart rate needs to be monitored .

• The medication is tapering off slowly over time can reduce your symptoms; if you take a low or moderate dose, you are less likely to feel withdrawal symptoms when you stop taking Adderall .

• Suppression of growth: Monitor weight and height in teenagers/pediatric patients during treatment .

Adderall may affect the growth rate, height and weight of children . Hence, the medication may be temporarily discontinued from time to time to avoid risk . This drug is not recommended for children under 3 years of age .

METHYLPHENIDATE (METADATE, DAYTRANA, CONCERTA, RITALIN)

What type of medication is Methylphenidate? Methylphenidate is a psychostimulant drug used for ADHD treatment . Even though these drugs stimulate the central nervous system, they have a relaxing effect on people with ADHD .

Ritalin, Concerta, Metadate and Daytrana are the common medications with this drug . Except Daytrana, all of these drugs are pills taken by mouth . Daytrana is in the form of skin patch (similar to Band-Aid) . Each day, the patch is applied to the hip region which delivers a dose of methylphenidate for 9 hours .

Methylphenidate may also be prescribed for narcolepsy, obesity and lethargy or fatigue .

What are the benefits?

1 . Improved Cognitive Function: It increases the level of dopamine neurotransmission in the brain which increases the capacity of attention or focus, raises motivation to work or objective-directed behavior .

This is especially beneficial for people who are unable to concentrate or suffer with impulsivity .

In patients of ADHD, Methylphenidate effectively allows normal cognitive functioning and reduces ADHD symptoms .

2 . Decreased Narcolepsy and Fatigue: In Narcolepsy, a person may suddenly go asleep, for example, even while driving .

Methylphenidate helps to reduce the symptoms of narcolepsy and reduce the fatigue and lethargy in patients where life had debilitated from normal working . 3 .

Weight Loss: Methylphenidate is used to treat obesity in patients who are dangerously overweight .

It causes an increase in the metabolic rate, heart rate, and suppresses appetite by simulating the central nervous system .

When used along with a comprehensive diet and exercise plan it can help obese people reduce fat effectively and improve health .

What type of dosage is usually recommended? Chewable tablets (Ritalin, Methylin, methylphenidate): Start with oral 10 mg, 2 or 3 times daily .

Take first dose half-hour before breakfast; repeat same at lunch, and a third dose between 2 and 4 PM, if required .

In general, the last dose should be taken before 6 PM . Doses may be increased by 5-10 mg weekly, up to a maximum of 60 mg/day . Transdermal system (Daytrana): Week 1: Apply 10 mg patch for 9 hour daily Week 2: Apply 15 mg patch for 9 hour daily Week 3: Apply 20 mg patch for 9 hour daily Week 4: Apply 30 mg patch for 9 hour daily Side effects of Methylphenidate The most common side effects are nervousness, sleeplessness, decreased appetite .

However, results may vary with patients as some children have reported improved sleep patterns with this medication .

Disordered or jerky movements may occur in about 9% of children .

Other side effects may include stomach pain, irritability, depression, headache, hair loss, and reduced spontaneity .

Symptoms of Overdose Common symptoms of overdose are confusion, hypertension, sweating, breathing difficulties, muscle twitches, vomiting, lethargy, agitation, psychosis, hallucinations, seizures, tachycardia, dysrhythmias (changes in heart rhythm and rate), hypertension, and hyperthermia .

Seek emergency care in case of overdose .

Warning and Precautions • Methylphenidate is addictive in nature .

• A person on methylphenidate should stay away from consumption of alcohol or drug abuse .

• It should not be taken by patients who suffer from severe arrhythmia, hypertension or liver damage .

• It should not be taken by patients who exhibit pronounced agitation, nervousness or addicted to drugs .

• Special precaution should be taken by individuals with epilepsy .

• Pregnant or breastfeeding women must inform doctor on taking Methylphenidate .

• There is risk of growth (height and weight) in children .

Type of medication Venlafaxine (Effexor) is an antidepressant licensed for the treatment of major depressive disorder (MDD), generalized anxiety disorder, and in certain anxiety disorders with depression, such as a person having suicidal thoughts .

Bupropion (Wellbutrin) is an atypical antidepressant and smoking cessation aid .

It is used to treat major depressive disorder and help people stop smoking by reducing craving and withdrawal effects .

Combination of Wellbutrin and Effexor may be effective at keeping a chemical balance that allows an ADHD patient to eventually become more mentally stable .

Type of ingredients Venlafaxine (Effexor): The active ingredient in Effexor in venlafaxine hydrochloride, a type of antidepressant known as SNRI or "serotonin and noradrenaline reuptake inhibitor" .

When these neurotransmitters are released from the nerve cells of the brain they tend to lighten the mood, which are also reabsorbed back by the nerve cells .

It is believed that depression occurs, when there may be lesser amount of serotonin and noradrenaline released from nerve cells in the brain .

Effexor acts on nerve cells in the brain by preventing the neurotransmitters serotonin and noradrenaline from being reabsorbed back into the nerve cells in the brain .

Bupropion: It is of common opinion that depression occurs with an imbalance of the amounts of neurotransmitters released in the brain .

Bupropion works as an antidepressant medication which affects the chemicals in the brain that nerves use to send messages to each other .

Recommended dosage Venlafaxine: Dose may vary for severity of depression and anxiety . The starting dose is 75 mg per day (divided into 2-3 smaller doses) . In general, the highest recommended total dose is venlafaxine 225 mg per day . In some exceptional cases, however, it can be 375 mg per day . Effexor can be taken with or without food .

Bupropion: For depression, the initial dose of immediate-release tablets is 100 mg twice daily, that may be increased to 100 mg 3 times daily (300 mg/day); maximum dose is 450 mg/day . The initial dose of sustained-release tablets is 150 mg daily; that may be increased to 150 mg twice daily, with maximum dose is 200 mg twice daily . The initial dose of extended-release tablets is 150 mg daily; that may be increased to 300 mg daily, with maximum dose is 450 mg daily . These tablets are administered once daily . Wellbutrin SR is given as two daily doses, while Wellbutrin XL is given as one dose daily . Side effects Common side effects are sexual dysfunction, nausea, somnolence, dry mouth, dizziness, insomnia, vomiting, numbness, sweating, confusion and anorexia . There can also be chest pain and increased blood pressure or hypertension, upset stomach or indigestion (dyspepsia), flatulence, weight loss . Recent reports indicate an increase risk of suicide .

Span of Venlafaxine (Effexor) and Bupropion Patients show improvement within the first 1-2 weeks .

Depressed mood and lack of interest in activities may need up to 6 to 8 weeks to improve fully . Who should be closely monitored? Caution needs to be taken with for people with glaucoma, neural (CNS) problems or any other mental illness, heart problems (high blood pressure etc) and pregnant or breastfeeding women .

What in case of missed dose? Take the missed dose when you remember, but if it is close to the next scheduled dose .

Do NOT take extra dose to make up for the missed one .

What in case of overdose? Seek emergency medical attention .

Overdose symptoms may include tremor, restlessness, muscle twitches, confusion, rapid breathing, hallucinations, aggressiveness, panic, tenderness or muscle pain, muscle weakness, flu or fever symptoms .

Other overdose symptoms include vomiting, nausea, diarrhea, uneven heartbeats, stomach pain, feeling light-headed, fainting and seizure (convulsions) .

Warning and Precautions • The medications must not be taken within 2 weeks of taking monoamine oxidase inhibitors (MAOIs) .

It can interact with other medications that increase serotonin (such as other antidepressants or migraine medications) .

• The medications can aggravate the effect of medications that can cause bleeding (such as ibuprofen and aspirin) .

• Stay away from consumption of alcohol or drug abuse .

• The medications should not be taken by patients who suffer from severe arrhythmia, hypertension or liver damage .

• The medications should not be taken by patients who exhibit pronounced agitation, nervousness or addicted to drugs .

• Special precaution should be taken by individuals with epilepsy .

• Pregnant or breastfeeding women must inform doctor before taking these medications .

• There is risk of growth (height and weight) in children .

What type of medication is Strattera? Atomoxetine (Strattera) is non-stimulant oral drug approved for the treatment of attention-deficit hyperactivity disorder (ADHD) .

It is a selective norepinephrine reuptake inhibitor (NRI) .

Strattera is available by prescription only, and not approved for major depressive disorder .

What are the benefits of Strattera? With Strattera, a person may feel more organized, from writing to using an agenda and do certain things easily that would otherwise have been very difficult .

For instance, a person can focus during workouts, take notes easily in lectures and concentrate on work better .

Strattera side effects; this med can be taken for an extended period with lesser risk of a side effects .

In many cases, lack of appetite, and hence weight loss is also reported .

What type of dosage is usually recommended? • In children and adolescents: The total daily dose should not exceed 1 .

4 mg/kg or 100 mg, whichever is less .

• For people up to 70 kg weight: Start with daily 0 .

5 mg per kg .

After 3 days, the dose can be increased to 1 .

2 mg/kg .

• Strattera may be taken with or without food, and can be discontinued without being tapered .

• Strattera capsules should be taken whole .

How long can an individual take this medication? In general, the pharmacological treatment of ADHD may be needed for extended periods .

Strattera can be carried out for extended periods with lesser risk compared to other powerful drugs, but the physician must periodically reevaluate the long-term effectiveness of the drug for every individual patient .

Strattera side effects what are they? In children and teenagers the most frequent side effects consist of: dizziness, mood swings, decreased appetite, tiredness, vomiting or nausea and upset stomach .

In adults the most frequent side effects consist of: decreased appetite, nausea, constipation, dizziness, dry mouth, sexual side effects, trouble sleeping, lack of sexual desire, and menstrual cramps .

Who should be closely monitored when taking? Strattera should not be taken if the person: • Has taken monoamine oxidase inhibitor or MAOI in the last 14 days .

• Suffers from glaucoma .

• Is allergic to Strattera .

• Suffers from a rare tumor called pheochromocytoma .

• Has serious heart-related problem that may worsen with the medication .

What in case of missed dose? Take the missed dose when you remember, but if it is close to the next scheduled dose .

Do NOT take extra dose to make up for the missed one .

What in case of overdose? Seek emergency medical attention .

Overdose symptoms may include tremor, restlessness, muscle twitches, confusion, rapid breathing, hallucinations, aggressiveness, panic, tenderness or muscle pain, muscle weakness, flu or fever symptoms .

Other overdose symptoms include vomiting, nausea, diarrhea, uneven heartbeats, stomach pain, feeling light-headed, fainting and seizure (convulsions) .

Warning and Precautions • The medications must not be taken within 2 weeks of taking monoamine oxidase inhibitors (MAOIs) .

It can interact with other medications that increase serotonin (such as other antidepressants or migraine medications) .

• The medications can aggravate the effect of medications that can cause bleeding (such as ibuprofen and aspirin) .

• Stay away from consumption of alcohol or drug abuse .

• The medications should not be taken by patients who suffer from severe arrhythmia or hypertension .

• The medications should not be taken by patients who exhibit pronounced agitation, nervousness or addicted to drugs .

• Pregnant or breastfeeding women must inform doctor before taking these medications .

• There is risk of growth (height and weight) in children .

• There can be suicidal Ideation in children and adults .

PSYCHOLOGICAL COUNSELING Counseling often comes to be of great help for adults with ADHD .

Counseling typically includes psycho-education (education about the condition) and psychotherapy (psychological counseling) .

Psycho-education can help the adult diagnosed with ADHD along with his or her family members to have a better understanding about ADHD and how it affects life and relationships; and information about the treatment .

Psychotherapy for adults diagnosed with ADHD tends to be focused on handling specific situations and develop the skills to solve certain problems: • Help out with ways to control temper • Make better relationships with friends, co-workers and family • Boost self esteem • Effectively deal with the social and academic failures happened in the past • Develop problems solving skills • Control impulsive behavior • Improve with organizational and time management skills Prevalent forms of psychotherapy to treat ADHD also include:

1 . Family therapy and marital counseling .

This is intended to help the people living with the person diagnosed with ADHD .

Living with an ADHD adult can put stress in relationships .

Being properly aware that the problems are not deliberate will help prevent blaming each other and improvise things better .

2 . Cognitive behavioral therapy - This structured form of counseling teaches the individuals on how to keep the behavior under control and feel optimistic in adverse situations .

It helps to cope with the effects of substance abuse, or mental conditions like depression, and attenuate relationships, work and school issues and other life challenges .

This therapy can be done on an individual basis or in a group .

HELPFUL SUGGESTIONS AND TIPS Symptoms of ADHD may vary with individuals, with each individual getting his or her own personalized course of treatment .

Here are a few tips that with help a patient suffering with ADHD to cope with daily work: • Prepare a list of things that are carried out frequently on a daily basis .

Avoid stress and overwork .

• Write down reminders and place them where the patient sees it often, e . g . in car, bathroom or over refrigerator .

• Maintain a planning calendar or appointment book to keep track of deadlines and appointments .

Electronic PDA (personal digital assistant) is a great device for such task .

• Keep a notebook at all times, so that any information available can be jotted down that can be reviewed later .

• Make a habit to store all information systematically in an organized way, whether on paper or as files in a computer .

• Split a large task into smaller ones .

• Request help from loved ones or family .

• Stick to the same routine on a daily basis .

RELATIONSHIPS ADHD has to be understood well, both by the affected person as well as the family members .

Lack of understanding between them can result frequent, unnecessary arguments that would give rise to psychological turmoil in the family .

Therapies to ADHD are specially focused to assist the person suffering from ADHD and the people associated with him or her .

There are classes that help in developing skills for better problem solving, develop communication skills and handle aggressive or provocative situations effectively .

ALTERNATIVE TREATMENT Alternative treatments can be an option to reduce the symptom of ADHD, some of these treatments are: • Special diet - Some foods can aggravate symptoms of hyperactivity include eggs, milk, wheat, caffeine and sugar .

Foods with additives and colorings should also be avoided .

Diet should carefully be monitored to check for and any eliminate any food (or element in food preparation) that exacerbate the symptoms of ADHD .

• Yoga and meditation - These activities help to relax the mind and body, and may assist in alleviating the symptoms of ADHD .

• Herbal supplements - There are claims with Chinese formulas that use gingko, ginseng and hypericum and other herbal remedies may help to treat ADHD, but such claims need to be well researched before use .

• Mineral or vitamin supplements - If a person is deficient or oversupplied with certain mineral or supplement, it can cause the certain symptoms to appear .

Such imbalances can be tested for, and corrected with proper mineral or vitamin supplements .

However there is no supplement yet known that would directly affect ADHD .

• Essential fatty acids - Omega 3 fatty acids are essential for the brain to work properly, omega-3 oils are usually available plentiful in seafood .

• Glyconutrients - It refers to eight sugars collectively believed alleviate ADHD symptoms by assisting in the production of an essential compound called "glycoprotein" .

• Nuerofeedback training - Also referred to as electroencephalographic biofeedback, a machine maps the brain wave pattern while the subject is made to perform or focus on particular tasks .

A person can monitor to control the patterns by examining the conditions that may alleviate or worsen the symptoms .

DEALING WITH IT AND GETTING SUPPORT Medications can help to treat an adult with ADHD, but other steps are also essential to understand and manage ADHD .

Some of these include: Administration - It may be tough for a person to inform his teacher or boss that he suffers from ADHD, but it is quite likely that they would make adjustments to make things more adequate for the sufferer .

Social support - People associated with the ADHD sufferer, such as colleagues, relatives and friends must also be well informed about ADHD and its consequences .

It needs to be understood that hyperactive actions committed by a person with ADHD may not be deliberate as it seems, but it is the outcome of a disorder .

It may be difficult to make other people understand, but this will make other people understand the situation better and improve relationships .

Support groups - With support groups, people with ADHD meets other individuals with the same condition and hence share information and strategies amongst themselves .

People with ADHD can meet other people directly or online .

PREVENTION ADHD is treatable, and when the disorder comes under control with appropriate counseling and treatment, steps must be taken so that the person does not revert back again to ADHD .

Consider the following steps to sustain and further improve the condition of person with ADHD: • Medications must be taken as instructed, and must be changed or discontinued only after consent from the doctor .

• The ADHD sufferer needs to positive to apply all the things learned, handle stress and adverse situations effectively and keep the things well organized .

• Seek help when required .

The people living with the person with ADHD disorder must be aware and understand the outcome of the disorder, and must help each other so that relationships remain good forever LIVING IN THE LEGAL WORLD It is quite normal for us to be quick to say what we feel, but most people filter the words in the process, so that the words don't offend anyone or community .

But an adult with ADHD would have less control over the speech, and in combination with abrupt changes in mood, impulsiveness and hyperactivity can lead to loss on job or face legal problems, or can even make the person with ADHD end up behind bars .

Take for example, an adult being scrutinized by a lawyer as a witness, plaintiff or offender .

The adult ADHD person may well be legal and strong on papers, but is weak with speech and impulsiveness .

If the lawyer intentionally puts questions that stir the mindset of the ADHD, the person may likely lose control in the court, a place where he or she can be arrested for contempt of court .

Another example is forgetfulness in maintaining legal papers and documents .

It is quite possible that a person with ADHD does not update the legal documents .

Take for instance, updating a driving license or a change in address .

Suppose a person with ADHD gets pulled over for a license check and the officer finds that the documents are not updated .

Most likely, in such circumstances, the person will get argumentative and confrontational because he or she cannot hold emotions in check that might end up in trouble for the ADHD affected person .

SENTENCING THOSE WITH ADHD The process involves answers to a number of core questions, such as: A .

The Offence • Seriousness of the offence • Triggers to the offence • Associated offences • Conditions suppressing the offence • Type of offence (e . g . sexual, violence) • Harm to the public by the offence B .

The Offender • Circumstances of the offender, including any mitigating factors • Welfare issues concerning the offender C . The Order and the Options • How to impose a specific order e . g . referral order .

• Risk of a young person offending again .

• Judgment based on all the evidence and reports (including view expressed by the offender and parents) most likely to prevent a person with ADHD from offending again .

• Is the judgment, that the court has in mind an appropriate punishment that is proportionate to the persistence and seriousness of the person's offending behavior? It is interesting to note in this regard, that people with ADHD are habituated to punishment .

Due to the characteristics of ADHD, mostly everything gets wrong all the way in their lives - maybe not in a criminal way, but probably in all other ways! People with ADHD are often punished consistently all of their lives, which makes them become more and more adapted to it .

It is difficult to punish a person who anticipates punishment and acclimatizes to whatever the punishment is being offered .

ADHD should not be used as an excuse to compulsive behavior, but if we are preparing to understand, it may explain the behavior .

ADHD INSIDE THE WORKPLACE ADHD is a condition where the individual gets disturbed with impulses of hyperactivity that affects concentration, causes forgetfulness and turns on an aggressive way of speaking .

Due to these factors, the individual very often faces problems at work which may cause him or her to be isolated from fellow co-workers, and even lose his or her job .

Reports indicate that due to factors affecting mental stability, an adult with ADHD works about 22 days less than non-ADHD employees in a year .

The World Health Organization reports that 4% of worldwide adults don't even realize that they are suffering with ADHD .

PROBLEMS WITH ADHD AT EXECUTIVE LEVEL An adult with ADHD symptoms at the management level can affect the working of an entire system .

We consider eight areas affected by such a condition:

1 . Organization skills .

This includes tasks from organizing their desk, to organizing specific tasks and skills, methodically prioritizing tasks, and systematically split big projects into smaller, doable ones .

2 . Farsighted planning .

An ADHD may lack the vision required to foresee circumstances at the management level .

This will have difficulty in predicting the situations that may arise with large projects having deadlines .

3 . Steadiness of work .

A person needs to constantly remain in focus until the assigned work is complete .

But a person with ADHD will face difficulty with concentration with lack of focus in the work process .

4 . Timing .

Many adults ADHD wait to the nick of time because of inability to comprehend instructions properly, or tend to delay work due to a similar, bad experience in the past .

This often makes them work in haste that further aggravates their condition, and prevents them to establish a work place .

5 . Determine Objective .

There may be difficulty in understanding the true objective of the work, the overall goal or actual target .

6 . Steadiness of mind .

There is difficulty in managing emotions, controlling temper, and taking responsibility for actions .

7 . Work with colleagues . A person with ADHD may be hesitant, not listen to others properly, unwilling to compromise and control temper .

This will directly destroy individual's decorum and affect his or her role as part of a team .

8 . Manage seniors . The boss can give advice or criticise for work . An adult with ADHD may become belligerent (aggressive), defensive, or lose temper in such circumstances .

CASE IN POINT An interesting legal battle took place between a physician name Robert Lewis and the University of Pittsburgh Medical Center (UPMC), where he worked .

An emergency room (ER) physician, for the University of Pittsburgh Medical

Center Dr . Lewis felt he suffered from ADHD and is work performance was hampered because of this .

So he requested permission to only see one ER patient, one at a time through the ER physicians department chief . The request by Dr . Lewis was turned down by the ER chief, instead he was put on probation on grounds of being distractible and also impaired, Dr . Lewis was also required by the ER department to submit to a mental assessment .

The evaluation/assessment resulted in Dr . Lewis being diagnosed with symptoms of ADHD . UPMC asked Dr . Lewis's mental assessment physician to make available most or all of the information pertaining to this case, which was refused by his doctor due to confidentiality requirements .

However, the treating doctor offered; which the University of Pittsburgh Medical Center hospital appear to have never followed up on to respond to certain questions .

Dr . Lewis was fired soon after on the grounds of: (a) Not providing letters from his mental assessment psychologist regarding his Attention Deficit Disorder diagnosis (b) Failing/not parking in the assigned doctors' parking spot (c) Holding on to unsigned paper documents for more than the allowed 30 days Dr .

Lewis responded by filing a lawsuit against UPMC, arguing that the hospital should have understood and accommodated his diagnosed ADHD behavior rather than firing him .

He filled under the law for Americans with Disabilities Act (ADA) .

The verdict: The court stayed with Dr . Lewis, saying that he had provided enough evidence to prove without a dough the hospital considered him disabled and as a result fired him due to his ADHD .

The defense argued that the hospital fired Dr . Lewis for the reason that he did not make available enough medical information .

This plea was turned down by the court, which said: Disabled employees, in particular those individuals with assessed psychiatric disabilities, might have a good explanation for not wanting to reveal every explicit detail (3/30/09 Dr

.

Lewis v . University of Pittsburgh Medical Center (UPMC) Bedford, W . D . Pa .) .

LESSONS LEARNED WITH THIS CASE 1 .

Don't look at each and every detailed aspect of any person who has requested a disability accommodation .

2 . Even a doctor may depend on another doctor's note on certain issues .

For instance, the emergency room chief should have given importance and consideration to the report of psychological evaluation of Dr .

Lewis, rather than going into each and every detail of Dr .

Lewis, which was brought to light by the court in the verdict .

3 . If a person informs their superior of their mental disability with a doctor's note, the supervisor should acknowledge and appreciate the fact and engage in a proper interactive process with the person, and sort out possible ways to handle the mental disability condition of that person .

LEGAL POINTS TO CONSIDER: Rehabilitation Act the most important Act of 1973 (RA) and also the Americans with Disabilities law Act enacted in 1990 (ADA) The legislative 1973 Rehabilitation Act (RA) restricts bias discrimination against any individuals with a known disability involving employment by the federal government, contractors who work for the federal government, or activities with federal financial support .

The Americans with Disabilities Act extends the same concepts stated in the RA to private employers, local and state governments, and places for example like public freely available accommodations, to include nearly all private schools in addition to institutions of higher education (institutions that are exempt from these laws are educational institutions that are controlled by religious organizations for example, that don't receive money from the government this law doesn't apply to them) .

It must be noted that involvement of money as damages or compensation is not covered in the above laws .

For instance, in the case of Trustees of the University of Alabama v . Garrett3, the Supreme Court maintained that seeking money damages under Title I (private employees) of the ADA, was barred by the Constitution . Similarly, some disabled students with suits for money damages were also turned down . To prevent misuse of the laws, it has been suggested that the RA and ADA does not require states to provide accommodations for individuals with disabilities, but to refrain from intentionally discriminating against them .

RA AND ADA WHO IS ELIGIBLE FOR BENEFITS UNDER THE LAW?
It is very important to understand that if an adult is diagnosed with ADHD, this diagnoses doesn't automatically make these individuals qualified for accommodations or protection under the Rehabilitation Act law (RA) or the Americans with Disabilities Act (ADA) law .

To be eligible, individuals have to meet four of these conditions according to the law: (1) Under the law these are individual people with disabilities .

(2) These individuals qualified without or with reasonable accommodations, for the position otherwise .

(3) These individuals are being disqualified solely for reason related to their disability from education or employment opportunity (4) These individuals are protected by the appropriate federal government laws .

These federal laws in essence require that institutions of higher education and also employers covered, should not show prejudice against persons who qualified but has a disability/disabilities .

Disability - An individual person under the law with a disability is described as: Any or every individual person who by the way has a mental impairment or physical impairment which significantly restricts one or possibly more than one of such individual's most important life activities, and has documentation of such an impairment, or those individuals are looked upon as possessing such an impairment .

Even though ADHD isn't specifically talked about in the rules, ADHD has been established in a lot of court trials as a " psychological disorder or mental disorder" and therefore is covered by the federal law .

Substantial Limits - Limits, the impairment impact have to be considerable, i . e . a major amount of impairment

To determine what is considered substantial the laws will compare a disabled individual with a normal average person in the general population to make a determination about what is considered substantial . If a person who is diagnosed with ADHD and is being treated for their ADHD with behavioral/psychological techniques or medication which allows them to effectively cope with their ADHD then these individuals will most likely no longer be considered qualified for the federal RA act law or the ADA act law .

And according to a Supreme Court ruling in reference to these individuals; who are cable of functioning in society, and taking into consideration the good and the bad effects of all the treatment they are receiving must be given access .

Most Important Life Activity - Under RA and ADA the most important life activities consist of: work, self-care activities, manual tasks, learning, breathing, walking, hearing, seeing and speaking .

Of these, the most important ones to an adult with ADHD is learning and working .

A . Learning - The impairment have to substantially limit the individual with ADHD, not just in a specific course of study, but in a broad area of learning .

A student in medical school argued that he felt anxiety taking physics and chemistry tests, and asserted that these feelings proved that enough evidence exist that prove that he suffers from substantial impairment when it comes to his ability to learn, but he was ruled against by the court .

The court ruled that mental impairment; like anxiety must be present in a broader assortment of live experiences, not just physics and chemistry .

B . Working - Let's take a look at working and impairment, in order to claim impairment the individual have to prove that it prevent them from being successful in numerous groups of jobs, not just one particular job .

Having a disability like ADHD must effect more than one aspect of that person's life, it's not only restricted to an individual work place .

Otherwise Qualified - It means that despite their disability, an individual would be eligible for an educational program (or job) provided they meet the basic requirements for a particular job or school program .

In a case that explains this condition, the employment termination of a neurologist with ADHD was upheld (maintained) by the court because he was considered a direct threat to his patients .

As he made errors in patient charts and dispensing medicine, the Court did not deem him qualified for the job despite his disability, and hence, he was ineligible for protection under the ADA .

HOW DO RA AND ADA APPLY IN THE WORKPLACE? In the workplace, there must not be discrimination when it comes to recruitment, upgrading, promotion, hiring, advertising and job application processes, award of tenure, transfer, leave, demotion, discharge, layoff, compensation, rehiring, and other benefits .

But to avail such protection, the employee needs to disclose the disability to the employer .

Such employees who are qualified for their jobs, but suffer with disabilities, may possibly be entitled for reasonable accommodations at the workplace .

But in most cases, it is not easy for the employee to prove oneself as qualified for the job, and at the same time establish that the major life activity is substantially limited .

This especially holds true where cognitive impairments are involved .

The accommodations sought by the employee must also be reasonable, which depends upon the kind of job .

To explain this, a senior-level executive with ADHD requested different accommodations, e . g . non-distracting workplace, a single supervisor, multi-staged tasks, written instructions etc; but they were turned down by the court with the ruling that executives at senior-level must be able to exercise independent judgment .

Such accommodations may be reasonable for junior-level employees but not for senior employees .

The accommodations sought by the employee must be specific .

For example, if an employer is not able to control all the factors that produce stress, he is not required to provide accommodation of reduced stress to the employee .

Moreover, acceptance by the employer depends upon the employee's assessment of stress level at any given time .

The employee must establish that the accommodations are an essential need due to his disability; the employee's desire for change may not be enough .

For example, an employee cannot be granted a day shift rather the night shift just because the employee prefers day shift .

The employee must prove that night shift is not possible due to the disability .

WHO WINS - EMPLOYER OR EMPLOYEE? The employees lose most of the cases because it is difficult to establish the substantially limited major life activity due to the disability, show the reasonableness of the accommodations, and at the same time prove oneself qualified for the job .

For an employee, it is important to consider the prospect of informally working out a mutually acceptable solution with the employer, many employers might agree to make reasonable accommodations, if they feel it improves the employee's performance .

Before taking legal action, an employee must carefully evaluate his or her legal position .

If a legal action is pursued, certified documents and records of the disability and the necessity for accommodations will be required .

Researchers say that adults who suffer with ADHD lose an average of $10,000 annually in income, or a whopping $77 billion annually on the national level .

Higher level jobs are hit more - the study shows that professionals with postgraduate degrees lose nearly $40,000 a year .

SELF ASSESSMENT The criteria as outlined by DSM-IV for attention deficit hyperactivity disorder was not put together with the adult in mind and is instead geared toward teenagers and children .

The adults that suspect that they may have this disorder can make use of a self assessment tool to decide with a great deal of accuracy whether or not they have ADHD .

This assessment tool or checklist as some prefer to refer to it is called the ASRS (Adult Self Report Scale) .

It was created by a set of experts in the field of ADHD headed by NYU's Len Adler and Harvard's Ron Kessler along with the WHO (World Health Organization) . Bear in mind however that it is only a screening tool . Even though this test only has six questions, it is rather accurate . One may wonder how accurate it is . Approximately eighty percent of the adults that had a positive score happen to be diagnosed with ADHD when they went to a doctor to do a more definitive diagnosis . In spite of this, for the individuals that get a negative scoring, it does not indicate that they might not have ADHD as the test is seventy percent sensitive .

To break it down a bit, this simply means that in a set of adults that are randomly selected, this test can only identify approximately seventy percent of the true instances of ADHD .

so if you happen to get a negative score and still have doubts, by all means go and get a full diagnosis done .

THE ASRS (ADULT SELF REPORT SCALE) TEST The appropriate responses are: Very Often Often Sometimes Rarely Never

1 . With what level of frequency do you experience challenges completing the last details of a task once the most difficult sections have been completed?

2 . With what level of frequency do you have issues organizing things when one is required to do so?

3 . How frequently do you experience challenges remembering obligations or appointments?

4 . Anytime you have an assignment that requires some level of deliberation, how frequently do you delay or avoid getting started?

5 . How frequently do you squirm or fidget with your feet and hands anytime you have to remain seated for extended periods of time?

6 . How frequently do you have the urge to just do something as if you had a built in motor? Stop and do the test before you read any further .

Write the answer which best outlines your situation .

Now on to the scoring process: For the first three questions if your answer was very often, often or sometimes award yourself a point for each .

This would indicate that if you stated often for question one and sometimes for questions two and three you would have earned three points .

No points should be awarded for answering rarely or never . For the remaining questions if your answer was very often or often you get a point for each . There are no points if the answer was sometimes, rarely or never . Add up all the points . If the total you get is four or more, you would have a positive score; should the score be three or less the score is negative . If your score was positive and you are prepared to get a full diagnosis done, make an appointment to see a doctor that specializes in ADHD .

Choose this physician based on the level of experience they have and not the number of degrees that they have Ask colleagues, relatives and friends if they can make a referral .

Heading to the correct doctor as soon as possible is vital as a lot of doctors are of versed in the nuances of this disorder and can make a misdiagnosis and prescribe incorrect medication which is potentially dangerous .

Typically, the medical practitioners that have the most training in this disorder are child psychiatrists and a lot of them treat adults as well .

Adult psychiatrists might not have a lot of training in the disorder while some internists and family doctors may be a bit more versed .

THANK YOU FOR PURCHASING MY BOOK Here's your chance to have a say in what future content is placed in this book .

I would like to make this section interactive by asking you for your suggestion on how I can make this book better for you and your fellow ADHD book lovers, leave a review .